Advance Praise for *Go Gentle Into That Good Night*

"*Go Gentle Into That Good Night* is not about death so much as it is about eternity . . . others have written about making friends with death. Boyd actually does it."

— Gretchen Haight
The Episcopal News

" . . . provides clear, practical advice about death and dying. The book empowers one to know what to do—to understand what action to take—when navigating the inevitabilities of death, both one's own and those of others."

— Bob Williams
The Episcopal News

What critics have had to say about the other writings of Malcolm Boyd:

"Boyd is a prophet for our times. All that is required of the reader is the ability to read—and the rudiments of a conscience."

— *The Christian Century*

"Malcolm Boyd wants to break down ghetto walls, tear off masks, remove barriers."

— *Book Week*

"Malcolm Boyd is a latter-day Luther or a more worldly Wesley trying to move religion out of the `ghettoized´ churches into the streets where the people are."

— *The New York Times Magazine*

"His experiences are moving and his concern is affecting."

— *The New Yorker*

"He is the saint of action."

— *Christian Science Monitor*

Go Gentle into that Good Night

Also by Malcolm Boyd

Crisis in Communication
Christ and Celebrity Gods
Focus
If I Go Down to Hell
The Hunger, the Thirst
Are Your Running with Me, Jesus?
Free to Live, Free to Die
Malcolm Boyd's Book of Days
The Fantasy Worlds of Peter Stone and Other Fables
As I Live and Breathe: Stages of an Autobiography
My Fellow Americans
Human Like Me, Jesus
The Lover
When in the Course of Human Events *with Paul Conrad*
The Runner
The Alleluia Affair
Christian: Its Meanings in an Age of Future Shock
Am I Running with You, God?
Take Off the Masks
Look Back in Joy
Half Laughing, Half Crying
Gay Priest: An Inner Journey
Edges, Boundaries, and Connections
Rich with Years

Go Gentle into that Good Night

by Malcolm Boyd

Genesis Press, Inc.
Columbus, Mississippi

Genesis Press, Inc.
406A 3rd Avenue North
Columbus, MS 39701-0101

GO GENTLE INTO THAT GOOD NIGHT

ISBN: 1-885478-48-8

Manufactured in the United States of America

First Edition

To
my mother
BEATRICE BOYD
1898-1997

Contents

Acknowledgments

I want to thank Bishop Fred Borsch of the Episcopal Diocese of Los Angeles for inviting me to be poet/writer-in-residence at the Cathedral Center of St. Paul in Los Angeles. And, Kristi Wallace and all my other colleagues and friends in that wonderful community.

Thanks to Wilbur Colom of the Genesis Press for wanting to publish this book, and handling it with loving care, and to Sylvia Baumgarten for brilliant, terribly honest, and incisive editing. Charlotte Sheedy believed in this book when no one else did, and guided its course.

A book is one of life's wonders. So much goes into the creation of it. I want to thank all those who contributed, in one way or another, to the making of this book. Since I share my life with him, my longtime life-partner Mark Thompson clearly played an indispensable role, for which I stand in eternal gratitude.

Introduction

Death grabs and holds my attention. I am fully aware there are no roadmaps, airline schedules or lists of recommended lodgings in eternity.

However, I wonder: Am I able to discover now any signs that will point me toward the route I shall travel? Can I follow any specific steps in order to prepare for my coming life in eternity?

These questions hold deep personal meaning for me. I am a healthy, hard-working, reflective, and vital man approaching seventy-five. Yet I hear unmistakable rumors that death is even now preparing invitations to a going-away party for me. Yes, in the future. But I gather a hall may have been booked, a caterer alerted.

Death hovers in other ways on the perimeters of my life. My life partner Mark at forty-five has the AIDS virus. Although he is taking protease inhibitors, which may garner him more time on Earth, he has a terminal illness.

At the opposite end of the age spectrum, I found my mother Beatrice. She resided in a nursing home when death claimed her ten days before her ninety-ninth birthday.

Eternity, where I'll go after I die, is as much a mystery to me as planets in their courses. I feel close to it, however, when I hike along ribbon-like dirt paths in the hills not far from my home. I see an eclectic pattern of numerous footprints in the dust. They belong to others like myself who trod here. I feel a strong sense of companionship with them. Are these strangers engaged in a search for meaning as I am? As pilgrims, we have a bond between us. Our spiritual pursuit in a touch of wilderness carries a yearning for something beyond the here and now.

I draw close to nature. Nothing is alien. Two coyotes stroll onto my path from nearby bushes one morning. Halting, we observe one another furtively, their shyness modifying an age-old image of menace. Having made peace with me, they depart unobtrusively into the landscape. Another day, as I turn a corner of my winding path, a long rattlesnake glides gracefully but firmly across it. I pay homage to its majesty by maintaining a respectful silence and distance.

Trees beckon like old friends. I assume they will change their form in eternity as I shall. Often I hold their branches in my arms, and have been known to talk to them. Above, the sky is open and seems to extend in endless directions. Here, freed momentarily from the routines of urban choreography, I feel a freshness and sense of freedom. It conjures up a wishful glimpse into eternity.

I do not expect its terrain (when I arrive there) to be hard or inhospitable. God knows we have already experienced so much of hell on Earth that I expect no repetition of it. As J. B. Priestley wisely observed, hell is neither fiery nor romantic, but gray, dismal, and just around the corner. I believe we have all experienced quite enough of it.

What of heaven? I like these words written by Fra Giovanni in 1513: "No heaven can come to us unless our hearts find rest in it today. Take heaven! No peace lies in the future which is not hidden in this present little moment. Take peace!" So, if we have not already experienced something of heaven, it is probably futile to expect much more of it in the future.

Whether we have a gold credit card or an undocumented worker's identification, eternity beckons to all of us quite democratically. Once there, it seems clear that after burial or cremation we will not possess the bodies we have now. But I firmly believe our souls will be intact.

This may actually provide a far, far better way to get to know people. While we were on Earth we excluded or included certain people solely on the basis of their bodies and outward appearances. This often led to terrible mistakes. We ignored, neglected or rejected a number of people simply because we didn't like their looks. They appeared too old or fat, too young or thin, too sophisticated or innocent. Maybe we didn't like their ethnic or racial identity. In any case, a superficial image has frequently provided a basis for acceptance or exclusion. Often we have succumbed to being attracted by women and men possessing stunning presence and physical beauty, yet whose souls resembled the spiritual nightmare of *The Picture of Dorian Gray.*

Consequently, getting along without our human bodies in eternity may prove to be a singular blessing. Some of us may even be astonished to discover for the first time what true love actually is.

Money, that maligned root of all evil, will be absent in eternity. No bank accounts, dollars, pesos, pounds, lira or francs. However, I am convinced good and evil will continue to co-exist. This means that spiritual growth, ever present here, will still be a major factor in eternity. As a result, there may even be a second chance to learn how to forgive someone or accept forgiveness. Too, we may find out how to love someone whom we called unlovable.

Death stands between us and eternity. It may come to us in a sudden, unexpected manner in a car crash or a fall from the sky. However, we may die peacefully in our beds at home, surrounded by loved ones in an ambience of tenderness and grace. Death, of course, is inevitable as a natural part of life.

Why not prepare for it now? Get ready to greet it as a friend and companion? The way is to live so fully and creatively, compassionately and joyfully, that our life and our death are alike.

"Do not go gentle into that good night," poet Dylan Thomas wrote. "Rage, rage against the dying of the light." Balderdash. Quite the contrary, let's prepare quietly and spiritually for the greatest spiritual adventure of our lives.

CHAPTER 1

Preparation for a Journey

If a human journey requires planning, it only makes common sense that our passage from this life into eternity needs at least an equal amount of preparation.

I was reminded of this when I took a journey recently to one of the hauntingly beautiful places in the world, the Monterey Peninsula of California and Big Sur. I rode horseback into the hills of Carmel Valley. The focus of the journey was to scatter the ashes of a beloved friend who had died of AIDS. Four of us made the trip. We had decided on a site located between two redwood trees. Stopping there, we held a brief ritual remembering our friend. We offered his body and soul to the universe he had inhabited. Then each of us took a handful of his ashes and scattered them in different directions near the trees.

Later during the journey I hiked and looked at giant

rocks washed by ocean waves in the bay at Point Lobos; watched sea otters resting on beds of kelp and sea lions playing lazily; shared companionship with Monterey cypresses and pine trees in a morning fog before the sun broke through.

Near the journey's end I stood in darkness one night on a hill in Big Sur. Looking up, I saw the stark drama of the galaxies, planets, and stars that crowded the sky. I was utterly overwhelmed by the sheer magnitude of them. Who could doubt eternity? I felt grateful and happy to be a part of the universe.

I was reminded that the most significant journey lies ahead. Of course, virtually no journey simply happens. My coming to Big Sur involved plane and hotel reservations, having a car, and packing necessary belongings (including hiking shoes and a sweater for foggy weather). An itinerary was a prerequisite. We cannot plan an itinerary for our ultimate journey, but we can prepare carefully for it in spiritual ways. Leave our earthly affairs in order. Allow peace to precede and follow us, instead of departing in chaos.

I will no longer be alive as an earthling by the year 2030. Does it seem odd to pronounce a death sentence for myself? Another way of looking at the situation is to say that I am simply accepting reality. But I wonder: Will I have achieved what I wanted during this life? Met my human responsibilities well? Will I be content finally to relinquish the reins of living here, and move on peacefully?

Mortality, a subject of near universal interest, has been addressed by countless authors and artists.

A certain imagery has emerged: gloomy, cold, morbid. One seldom identifies mortality with warmth, sunlight, brightness. *Must* it be so awful? The fact is, time will run out. Or, as it's often put in the vernacular of the media, the tape is rolling. What, if anything, can we do about it?

The best answer for me is: Live as fully in the present as possible. Don't delay significant decisions by placing them in the future. Start, or lovingly maintain, the relationship you want. Do the work you want. Paint the picture, shoot the photograph, compose the music, write the book. What are the things you'd like to do, but haven't? The time is now. Ramana Maharshi asked: "Why do you want to know what you will be when you die, before you know what you are now?"

Life is a rich feast. It seems a mortal sin to make it dull as dishwater, and have no vision or hope. Time places definite limitations on us. However, we can—and must—work creatively within these limitations. Kick over the traces. Risk. Be imaginative. Sometimes even do what is clearly unimaginable. I discovered this early in life.

In high school I lacked glamour. What could I do about it? I didn't have any money, know how to dance, or drive a car. Not surprisingly, no young woman was dying to go out with me on a date. Drastic remedies were called for. I visited a local bookstore and found a book that taught one how to dance. It diagrammed the steps for a variety of well known styles, including the waltz and the tango. Since I could not afford to buy the book, I jotted down all the steps in my school notebook.

At home I went into my room, closed the door, turned on the radio to the music of Glenn Miller and his orchestra, and tried out the steps. I learned them by heart to the beat of "Sunrise Serenade," "Tuxedo Junction," and "In the Mood." Then I asked a friend with a car if I could double-date with him. Finally, I approached the most beautiful coed in school and invited her to go to the year's top dance with me.

Connie was her name. She had just broken up with the captain of the football team and president of the student body. So, miraculously, she was without a date for the dance. She said yes. She wasn't just beautiful. She was gorgeous; sexy, tanned, voluptuous, a great wit, and could dance. We were the Fred Astaire and Ginger Rogers of the evening, to the total surprise of everybody, including the captain of the football team, who kept looking at her with longing in his eyes. But she had eyes only for me. I had no interest whatsoever in the future; the present was perfect.

Time catches us where, as, and how we are. I remember when a friend telephoned to tell me she had just been fired from her job. She'd been under the impression she was doing good work. Later, she found her dismissal had no connection to her work, but was simply a bureaucratic policy decision. She was ordered to leave her office and desk *now,* not permitted to clean out her desk or tell co-workers goodbye. Her employer said she could come back alone that night and get her personal things.

No warning or preparation.

Another friend learned in approximately two minutes that his marriage of twelve years was over. The realization, break, and decision hit fast, without even the luxury of finding a moment's refuge in detachment.

Undoubtedly, there had been signs of warning, but there was no preparation.

Yet another friend sat inside a doctor's office and received the diagnosis of a serious illness in an abrupt thirty seconds. There was no place to hide. Absolutely no way to make this shattering news go away.

The time had come, as we say.

There are different ways to respond to such dramatic immediacy. One can accept despair or numbness, even become self-destructive and try to obliterate reality. Or, one can check out alternative courses of action, live in the moment, and choose life.

My friend who was fired from her job chose the latter way. She stopped crying over spilled milk, went job hunting, then decided on self- employment. She solicited clients, networked with other people, and kept up her momentum, spirits, and energy.

Here is what happened to the two people in the marriage that shattered. After counseling, they realized that they wished the best for each other because, although no longer in love, they acknowledged a permanent bond of caring. They decided to avoid inflicting further hurt on one another, and to move from pain and despair to commencing new lives.

My friend who sat in the doctor's office undertook recommended treatment that extended her life. Now she does not plan beyond five years ahead. She is serene, peaceful, and has started projects she had always desired. She cultivates her friends, enjoys her home, has discovered the joys of travel, and has established a deep spiritual base in her life.

Life is so short.

We have, at best, only a few decades. I didn't realize this for a long time. When I turned thirty, it seemed the end of the world. I was old, I told myself. Forty slipped by with deceptive ease; I recalled the title of an old bestseller, *Life Begins at Forty*, and took comfort from its hopeful suggestion. A number of my friends at that time were older men and women. I respected them, enjoyed their company and wisdom, and found their easy charm and ingrained humor a delight. Their age seemed altogether natural. I was at ease in their company.

Fifty, however, was a nightmare. I didn't seem to belong or fit anywhere. I was neither young nor old, and had trouble defining myself. I realized with a start that I hated being fifty. A major reason is that I was, to my surprise, inexplicably afraid of growing old. So, I did something absurd and completely out of character. I bought black hair dye at a store, carried it home, and applied it to my graying hair. Then, looking into a mirror, I did not see a desired image of a handsome, youthful, virile miracle of transformation. I saw myself. Yet paradoxically, I gazed at a stranger whom I did not like at all. Instantly I wished to get back to my own peppery, graying hair as quickly as possible. When I did, I sincerely liked it. Did I also like *me*? Yes. I focused gratefully on a dawning awareness that it was all right to be growing older. I was glad to be myself.

By the time I reached sixty, I was philosophical, seasoned, and quite content. Seventy was a lark. I have found that decades are the most appropriate markers of time for me. When we see our life measured this way, we recognize its clear limitations in terms of time, as well as positive actions we can take. For one thing, we can treat death and dying as a point in the life cycle, a final season we are growing into and preparing ourselves for. (We can do this at any age; many persons with AIDS have managed to do this courageously and gracefully when they were young). We can try to improve the quality of life. Gandhi pointed out that it is beneath human dignity to lose one's individuality and become a mere cog in the world's machinery. We can remind ourselves of this and assist others who are victims.

Sometimes when we can't slow down time's rigid, relentless movement, we can at least slow down ourselves. If we feel we're trapped in time ("I can't be myself in this situation"), then we can break free, managing to be authentic in the time remaining. A corollary of this is to be ready to embrace change. Don't stay locked inside past attitudes and customs and demands.

Forgiveness of self is of paramount importance. I have wrestled with this for years. When it comes to memories, I've had a tendency to replay old tapes of reminiscences in my head. Old fears. Old problems. Old failures and embarrassments, real or imaginary. Even some highly dramatic scenes with outbursts of rage, and searing moments of shame, repeated again and again. When I do this, I haunt myself. Not content to let the past be the past, I allow it to intrude on the present. This is silly and dangerous. In his book *Homecoming,* John Bradshaw declares that the healing of our memories resembles the forgiveness of sins. Illuminate the present. Turn the lights on. Accept forgiveness and healing. Be willing to live.

Such willingness can extend to death, when it comes. Be open to its experience. Do not fear it. Understand the links between living and dying, dying and living. In *The Mambo Kings Play Songs of Love*, Oscar Hijuelos wrote: "He walked among the tombstones and felt exhilarated, talking to the spirits." The dead (who are living) are with us. Death itself is not archaic, remote, or what we call a dead object.

Walt Whitman had some very loving things to say about death in "When Lilacs Last in the Dooryard Bloom'd":

> *Come lovely and soothing death . . .*
> *praise! praise! praise!*
> *For the sure-enwinding arms of cool-*
> *enfolding death.*
> *Dark mother always gliding near with*
> *soft feet,*
> *Have none chanted for thee a chant of*
> *fullest welcome?*
> *Then I chant it for thee . . .*

This is a wonderful, freeing paean to death. Death is not seen as forbidding, horrible, an enemy, a scourge, a curse, or the ultimate nightmare. Death is seen here as natural, lovely, soothing, gentle, comfortable, and welcome.

In a famous poem by Emily Dickinson, death is seen as a courteous gentleman-caller, perhaps middle-aged, kindly and attentive:

> *Because I could not stop for Death—*
> *He kindly stopped for me—*
> *The carriage held but just Ourselves—*
> *And Immortality.*
> *We slowly drove—He knew no haste*
> *And I had put away*
> *My labor and my leisure too,*
> *For His Civility—*

Here, death is seen as kind, attentive, considerate, decent, civil, warm, and leisurely. What a change from an image of death as intrusive, imperious, selfish, arrogant, demanding, unyielding, and cruel. St. Francis of Assisi referred to death as "my brother." These views of death are so much more helpful than negative words and images. If we can accept the blessing of death as a part of the blessing of life, then it becomes possible for us to integrate the concept of death into our understanding of living.

As our life's journey ends, how can we prepare for eternity?

We must rely on intuition, imagination, and faith. Anglican mystic Evelyn Underhill, in her book *Worship,* wrote that the reality and attraction of God's eternity must be experienced in time itself, if they are to enter and transform our experience.

This may involve a number of different things. For example, participation in liturgy and public worship. Private prayer and meditation. Love of nature. Awareness of serendipity. Realization that what we see with our eyes can be quite incomplete: We need more.

Photographer Richard Avedon described how he began trying to create an out-of-focus world, with a heightened reality better than real. When he took off his glasses, especially on rainy nights, he got a more beautiful view of the world than twenty-twenty people get. He wished to reproduce this more poetic image that he privately enjoyed. In doing so, he reached a deeper-than-surface level of reality.

I follow a poetic approach when it comes to eternity. For example, here are two images that conjure up for me meanings I associate with eternity.

The first depicts the immense sweep of a beach at sunset. There is no human or animal figure in the scene. Hills and mountains that fill the background are a soft gray. The sky overhead has clouds, both light and dark. The sea is silver, the land on its edge black. A sense of serenity and peace is communicated. There is absolutely no movement; only an awesome, spellbinding stillness. Three archetypal forces are here: sky, water, and land. Nothing individual or characteristic stands out from these. If I were present in the scene, I believe that I'd be less conscious of self, and more aware of myself as part of a greater community. More to the point, I believe I'd be utterly absorbed in a pervasive force of unity. Yet I would still be myself, engrossed in a peace so immense, deep and fulfilling, that it would simply enfold me.

The second image is of a cave. I am looking into it from outside an entrance. I see a stairway with steps leading upward. At the far end of the cave appears yet another entrance, and directly beyond it I see another stairway going up. I seem to be looking at part of what I can only describe as a labyrinth. Here, I realize I would have ample time for quiet meditation and reflection. However, a sense of aloneness, even isolation, disturbs me. My need of a community of like-minded people to associate with intrudes on my consciousness. Could I find wholeness, perhaps as a result of exploring the labyrinth? Climbing the mysterious steps? Waiting patiently for someone to come? It is possible a community is honeycombed within the cave. This could mean continuity, warmth, and involvement.

Yet what if it did not? It occurs to me: I may not need continuity, warmth, and involvement (as I understand them) in eternity. It seems I have to be ready to give up preconceptions of all kinds. Give up control, finally and completely. Prepare for God's action, not my own.

A glimpse into eternity can occur in the midst of everyday life. A deep revelation of truth, shocking as a sudden view of a mountain range from a train window, lasts only a moment, yet can be remembered for a lifetime.

My brushes with eternity come when I am removed momentarily from the energy of speed, a crowd, a deadline. In the absolute, incomprehensible silence of a mountain range or a desert. In the total blackness of night when there is not a single ray of light. In the first lightness (or just before it) of dawn. In a moment of surface reflection by a lake or a stream, when I gaze into its depth and study the surface reflection of trees, and feel a strong pull into its center where (I know) there exists another world. Yet I have also brushed against eternity on a crowded street where, to my surprise, I have seen a Christ-figure in a stranger, perhaps a homeless person.

A recent encounter with eternity seemed so natural that, when it happened, I smiled in recognition. I visited a hospital to have a series of x-rays taken at the request of my physician. A technician explained the pictures he needed and what he required of me. Then he vanished for a few moments after taking a set of x-rays, in order to ascertain if they were all right.

I was alone in that small room inside the immense hospital, and the situation seemed surreal. Silence swelled inside the space, yet it seemed to have a curiously noisy edge. I was anything but relaxed, yet felt detached and out of context. An appointment I had the next hour seemed as distant as the moon. Nothing really mattered very much. After all, I was helpless—stripped and then garbed in a funny hospital garment with the back wide open—lying on a table that seemed as impersonal as a slab. How long would it be before the technician returned? Since this was a hospital, why couldn't I hear ambulances or sirens, or the sound of doctors and nurses rushing along corridors, or someone crying? A massive, spooky, Spielberg-like x-ray machine looming over my body resembled nothing so much as a grotesquely playful dinosaur.

Then, in that unnatural silence, I brushed against eternity. It seemed generous, encompassing, accepting, welcoming. Although I was alone, I felt a part of everything. The x-rays seemed inconsequential; what difference did it really make? I was *at home;* there was nothing to fear, and in that moment I could easily have faced into eternity and gone with it without even saying goodbye. I was far, far away when I heard the technician's voice: "The x-rays are fine. You can go now."

In fifteen minutes I was speeding on a nearby expressway toward my appointment. My day moved in a not unfamiliar pattern. I was back into speed, high energy, crowds, noise, and deadlines.

Just then a speeding car veered dangerously onto the expressway from a ramp and would have collided with me if I hadn't been able to turn swiftly into the lane to my left. There, mercifully, no other car lurked.

Nobody knew I had brushed against eternity. But I did. An appointment with it lay ahead. Would I be prepared?

CHAPTER 2

The Greatest Value

Do many people allow death entirely too much self-importance? Let it strut like a dictator, be scarier than a horror movie, get away with more tricks and illusions than the Wizard of Oz?

I asked several friends to engage in a project with me. To sit down in a quiet place, put on their thinking caps, take pen and paper in hand, and write exactly what they honestly felt about death. Just that. No games or pretense.

Their responses indicated they feared death to an incredible degree. It angered and frustrated them. They appeared to grant it a disproportionate amount of control over their thoughts. This is a part of what they wrote.

"Damn it, I don't want to be helpless, in agony. I don't want to be grabbed out of life suddenly with no warning and no chance to say my goodbyes. Death is an ugly presence in my life, a witch wearing a bad mask."

In my view, this response cries out for a radical change. Don't *allow* death simply to be an ugly presence. Start working to demythologize death.

"I see death as a monster with a voracious appetite. It made my mother cry and have nightmares. My father feared death so much that he sought relief in the world of business and success. I run from death. I have horrible fantasies about my own death. Its existence precludes my living a full life."

But it's not going to do any *good* to run from death. Death is a reality. Better to move with purpose toward it. Get acquainted. Do some serious inner work to prevent its getting in the way of your life.

"Fuck you, death. Get away from me. I don't want you. Just get away. I don't want anything to do with you. Fuck you. I hate you."

This isn't going to work as a form of exorcism. Death is not going away.

"Death causes me to shrink and go unconscious. It is

too terrible and uncompromising. I cannot control it at all. It will come and finish my life experience whenever it wants, and I am powerless unless I commit suicide."

This grants death a power that is absurd and irrational. (We will discover in the pages of this book numerous ways to deal with death and prepare for it.) What's needed is creativity, hope, faith, and common sense. And a lot of humor.

"Death looms before me every time I step on an airplane. As long as I am on solid ground, I feel some sense of control. In the air I am in death's territory. I often imagine what my relations felt and thought as they went to the gas chambers."

The air is no more death's territory than solid ground is. Death didn't place people in gas chambers; Nazis did. Don't give death a power it never had.

"Why do I feel so ambivalent about death, caught in a love/hate attraction/ revulsion? To embrace what is most horrible, to repel what is most desirable. I ache for the trust, the faith, to close my eyes and fall backward, with no doubts, no fear, no questions."

There is considerable wisdom here. And awareness of the deep ambiguities in many of our feelings about death.

"Death is so demanding. It wants to capture me like a lover used to. Being in love cracked me open to my core. I resist death in the deeper places. Will I allow myself to come into a relationship with death with all my being?"

This is an extraordinarily basic question, it seems to me. It gets to the heart of the matter. For death is neither casual nor partial.

"I lost my husband. I feel we never said goodbye the week he knew he was going to die. Neither one of us had the courage to talk about it. We were both too afraid of death to be open and honest."

This is quite understandable, yet still very sad. Hopefully others who find themselves in a similar situation will find the necessary courage.

"Yes. I'm afraid of death. Yes. I'm confused by it. In a split second in the future will I become an 'It's dead, that body over there'? It seems so impersonal and therefore brutal."

It need not be impersonal at all. Or brutal. However, if we foolishly determine that it must, then our attitude can affect our demise.

Other friends I've known have found both solace and meaning at the time of death. At thirty-five, Scott

had red hair, expressive hands that he used energetically
to make a point, and AIDS. He told me: "I have night
sweats. Chills and fever. Diarrhea. I only feel human to
six p.m. My next goal is to have a wonderful, beautiful
death. Life isn't just la-de-da happiness. It is also darkness. The basis of Christianity is Jesus on a cross. You
don't get Easter without Good Friday. I feel God knows
what my needs are. Jesus is a guy I want to hang out
with."

Dave was also a casualty of AIDS. Months before his
death, we shared a jail cell after our arrest for civil dis-
obedience to protest inadequate services for AIDS. As
empty hours dragged on, day turning to night, we talked
in our cell about existential matters that lay on his mind
and soul. He explained that his spirituality was rooted in
Buddhism and Taoist reflection.

"I still have a lot of fear about dying," Dave told me.
"One of the most reassuring things is when I genuinely
feel a higher power moving in my life in a benevolent,
intelligent way. Then I feel complete confidence come
over me. It's O.K. when solutions come up, doors open,
and I sense a condition of rightness. This causes me to
feel less frightened about what the aftermath of death

might be. In other words, what is carrying me is not going to drop me."

By his own words, Dave felt security as he approached dying. Many others, facing death, do not. Of course, a vast number of people do not experience a sense of security in facing life itself.

Here's an example of it.

Actress Gloria Swanson's career peaked in 1925 when she earned seven thousand dollars a week and became the Marquise de la Falaise de la Coudraye. Swanson's mother told her this should be the happiest time in her life. However, the actress replied: "No, Mother, it's the saddest. I'm just 26. Where do I go from here?"

In a world of present shock and constant change, a basic question stands out: What is security? What is there to save? One's bank account? Stocks and bonds? One's soul? Which will accompany us from death into eternity?

We hear a world-weary commentator's views on this in the biblical Book of Ecclesiastes. If he lived today, he might be an acerbic essayist or critic. He's worked hard, grant him that. Yet he knows he cannot keep his reward, prestige, and treasure. He will have to leave his riches to someone who will come after him.

What a blow to an ego. Yet none of us, not even the Queen of England, the King of Spain, or the President of the United States, has a buffer against this fate. Someone else will become mistress or master! Ecclesiastes feels it is a harsh fate, an unfair predicament. What is left for humanity after all the stress, toil, and strain? Our years are full of pain, our work is vexation, our dreams troubled. All is vanity.

Of course, we leave everything material behind. However, isn't that a sort of blessing? Who would want to carry heavy boxes, the accumulated possessions of a lifetime, art objects, books, trunks, safe deposit boxes, and familial mementoes into eternal life? Don't we wish to be ready to get involved in a new life without a lot of burdens ?

My own mother's story taught me more about this than all the books of wisdom in the libraries of Harvard and Yale, Stanford and Michigan, possibly could.

Always, Beatrice had been one of those women in the Katharine Hepburn lineage: independent, strong-willed, utterly decisive, unsentimental, disciplined, on top of her game, a self starter, every inch a lady but dispensing with fools fairly rapidly (without hurting their feelings), and honest to a fault. She never smoked or drank, ate sensibly, swam daily, loved dogs as her pets, maintained correspondence with friends, talked on the telephone every day to a group of women close to her, painted her own Christmas cards, watered her roses, and talked back with passion to Dan Rather on the CBS Evening News when his reports did not fall in line with her strong political opinions.

All this went very well until Mother's age started to show itself more starkly after she turned ninety. For one thing, she had to give up driving her car. This cut sharply into her independence. When she could no longer shop regularly at a grocery, Meals-on-Wheels began delivering her a nutritious noonday meal.

Various signs pointed to new problems. An earlier eye cataract operation had helped her sight, but now it was deteriorating again. Her memory wavered, along with her motivation and energy. Her physical condition weakened noticeably and, although she had a cane, she seldom used it while walking around her house. (Yet once I found her climbing a stepladder in the yard to pick oranges). Mother refused to use a walker, to consider moving into a retirement facility, and to allow someone to come into her house to clean or be of assistance. Beatrice was adamant about these things, stubborn and even abrasive, and the strength of her personality and conviction served to prevent me from circumscribing her wishes.

One afternoon during a visit, I was in the backyard as she stood at the other side of it. I saw her fall. I ran to her, lifted her, and placed her on a deck chair. I was aware something irrevocably bad had occurred, and was prepared to call 911 when Mother asked "Can't we just sit here for a while, be quiet and rest?" I knew we could not. Shortly, an ambulance arrived and carried her to the emergency room of a nearby hospital. Surgery was necessary for a broken hip and a broken elbow. It became apparent she would never see or walk inside her home again.

After two months in various hospitals, primarily for rehabilitation purposes, Beatrice needed to be placed permanently in a nursing home where she could receive twenty-four-hour medical and nursing attention. Suddenly, I realized there was no one but me to make not only this decision about her life, but a number of others.

What could I do? A human life was in my hands. What would be best for my mother? Decisions had to be made quickly. I needed, in fact, to make huge ones about the various aspects of a loved one's entire life. I found a nursing home, fortunately one that proved to be caring, exemplary, and splendid.

Then I had to strip Beatrice's house of a lifetime's possessions. I spent long hours emptying closets and drawers of papers, underwear, photographs, souvenirs, memorabilia, hats, dresses, shoes, coats, pots and pans, pharmaceutical items, scarves, dishes, books, seashells, letters. Whenever I seemed to make progress, a fresh batch of things appeared. Depressed and emotionally exhausted, I lay on a bed, memories intruding on my consciousness, wondering how I could complete such a task.

This acutely reminded me of visits a number of years before that I had made to another old woman in a nursing home. At eighty-eight, all the possessions of her life had been reduced to the contents of two cardboard boxes beneath her bed. They held, among other things, her marriage certificate, photographs of her children and their families, letters from her deceased husband during his military service, a favorite prayer book, and a wedding band that had belonged to her mother. Charlotte Watson Sherman wrote in her story "glory" in *When I Am an Old Woman I Shall Wear Purple:* "you know i never thought i'd be able to pack up all my life and put it in a paper bag. all my life in a paper bag."

In a convalescent hospital, Beatrice resided in a room with two other women. In that small space she had only a very small table with two tiny drawers beside her bed to hold her possessions. These included a hairbrush, a toothbrush, a prayerbook (which she could not read any longer), a copy of a book I wrote inscribed to her, and cards from friends. Hanging on the wall near the foot of Mother's bed was a cork board that held a small oil painting she had done forty years ago, two fifty-year-old pictures of her mother, a black-and-white photograph of me, a color photo of me swimming at a beach in Hawaii, a Halloween card showing a funny black cat, a copy of a magazine article I had written about her entitled "How To Be a Survivor," and a tiny cushion with the words "Mothers Are Special People."

What struck me most about Beatrice's life in the nursing home was the way she had chosen to deal with the new realities of her life. The change was absolute. She had lost the last vestige of independence, becoming an almost totally dependent person. Before, she had lived alone in a controlled environment; now she was part of a tightly knit community of patients and nurses. Previously, her TV viewing had been limited to the evening news; now a TV set was turned on and played loudly many hours of the day, although she seemed oblivious to it and seldom even glanced in its direction.

Since she was shielded in no way from the often hard realities of inhabiting a nursing facility, it seemed to me that Beatrice reflected what Stephen Levine wrote in *Who Dies?*: "Clearly, a practice that would be useful is to cultivate an openness to what is unpleasant, to acknowledge resistance and fear, to soften and open around it, to let it float free, to let it go."

Elisabeth Kubler-Ross identified five changes that she believed are experienced by people who are dying. I noticed how my mother, although not yet literally dying but certainly approaching death, seemed to identify with these changes too. At first, there was denial: "I suppose I'll be going home soon. I'm fine. There's nothing the matter with me."

Then came anger: "I hate this place. Someone tried to strike me. Why don't you get me out of here?" There was bargaining and depression. During this period she fell out of bed onto the floor of her room three times at night when she tried to climb out and get away. For her safety (it would have been a disaster for her to break her hip again) I gave permission for Mother to be restrained in her bed and wheelchair. This bothered me as much as anything else that had happened; it seemed unfair, cruel, and nightmarish. But soon this was no longer necessary. Beatrice valiantly came to acceptance of her condition.

"This is it, isn't it?" she asked one day. I allowed as how it probably was. She adjusted rapidly to that reality, choosing to discover contentment, even happiness. To my delight, Beatrice made friends with several women like herself who were confined to wheelchairs in the home. They visited, talked, and shared a life largely hidden from my understanding. Beatrice said she had no fear of death, and would welcome it; but until it came, she felt content, grateful for her care and surroundings, and remarkably vital as a person.

In John Updike's novel *In the Beauty of the Lilies,* Grandfather Wilmot says: "I don't expect anything of dying but I never expected too much of life." The key to understanding my mother's attitude toward death is her long, tender embrace of life.

She was born in 1898; her life came close to spanning the twentieth century. Her faith was simple, honest, and uncomplicated. At the age of twenty, she revealed an openness to the needs of others that would continue for the rest of her life. When a deadly influenza epidemic raged in 1918 during World War I, Beatrice volunteered to teach and care for Navajo Indian children on a reservation in Arizona. If they died in the night, she buried their small bodies in the desert. She was a forerunner of those who, in a later generation, would serve in the Peace Corps.

Beatrice worked for most of her life. From 1950–59 she served as parish secretary in a church. I found this letter written to her by the women of the parish on the occasion of her departure: "You have been our sounding board, our wailing wall, our fellow-sufferer when we were upset, and our joint exulter when we were happy. You have carried the ball for us when we became too timid or discouraged or worn down. A rare privilege has been ours, sharing the friendship of the finest person most of us will ever know."

At seventy, Mother retired, and immediately began volunteer work as a teacher at the Childrens Hospital of Los Angeles. One day a small boy who was a patient said to her: "You're old, aren't you?" "Yes," she replied. "Good," he said, "then I can talk to you."

After Beatrice fell and broke her hip at the age of ninety-five, and entered the nursing home, the journey of her soul became her bedrock. It was not something ephemeral or other-worldly, but rooted in all the muck and glory of life as she experienced it on a daily basis.

Earlier, when she lived in her own home, she had worked in her garden and dug in the soil, and cared for her goldfish in an outdoor pond. She also painted canvasses and Christmas cards, wrote stories, kept a journal, and studied French and the guitar. Now, residing in the nursing home, her patience involved more than waiting. It included endurance. I noted how she retained the gut courage to greet others with a genuine smile, and was completely grateful for her life.

When its end was approaching, I was notified by her doctor. Then she contracted pneumonia. Her behavior throughout the dying process reminded me of these words written by psychotherapist Irvin D. Yalom in *Love's Executioner:* "I have always felt that the way one faces death is greatly determined by the model one's parents set."

Beatrice set a model. Shortly before her death, I was alone with her. She had been close to death for two days. Now, she lay on her bed, eyes shut, breathing laboriously through her open mouth, showing no sign that she was aware of anything. I placed my left hand on her forehead. My right hand took hold of her hand, which was limp. I said, "Mother, I love you. You are in a long corridor. At the end of it you see light and angels, God and people who love you. It is time to go now. You are surrounded by love. Let go, dear."

In just a few moments her hand slipped out of mine. But then, almost immediately, that same hand took the initiative by firmly clasping mine. Then Beatrice's eyes opened and she focused clearly on my face. After a moment, her eyes closed for the last time. However, she continued to hold my hand, decidedly and with strength, for several minutes. Finally, her hand slipped out of mine. There was no communication after that. She died two hours later.

The next morning, driving my car in the rain, I felt numb and tired. Suddenly I experienced a lightness. My mother seemed to speak to me: "You told *me* to look for the light and the angels and God! I did. I found them. Now, why don't you? They're here."

Beatrice's spiritual devotion and religious faith were matched only by her honest, lively sense of humor. For her, the emperor wore no clothes. She was the least phony person I ever met. For her, all the world was a stage, and she participated fully in the drama.

Several years ago I was asked, as an exercise to compile a list of people I admired. The implication was that they would be illustrious or famous. Initially I thought this would be an easy thing to do. However, staring at a blank paper before me, I realized how few people I actually admired.

I was in a workshop conducted by my friend Richard N. Bolles, author of *What Color Is Your Parachute?* Suddenly it dawned on me. The women and men I admired were those who lived for others, not merely for careers, bank accounts, egos, and curtain bows. My list included Rosa Parks, Dag Hammarskjold, Eleanor Roosevelt, St. Francis, Florence Nightingale, and Nelson Mandela.

Beatrice seemed to understand such people, their goals and motivations. Although Mother was never on the cover of *Time,* a star in a film, or an occupant of high political office, she was outstanding, in my view, and seriously worked at her lifelong task of becoming a value bearer.

CHAPTER 3

How Can I Get from Here to There?

How many deaths must we die?

We must die voluntary deaths until we die.

What is the difference between death and deaths?

Our *deaths* are of the spirit, affecting our pride, our isolation, our spiritual murdering and exploitation of others, our greed and envy. Our *death* is in the body as well as the spirit, and marks our physical annihilation on Earth.

How are deaths related to death?

Voluntary deaths diminish our egoism and multiply our open relationships with other people, increase our awareness of the universe and life surrounding our own personal realms. When we have become accustomed to dying—or living in a broader and deeper sense—we are naturally adjusted to the final act of death itself, which is an act of life.

How are the acts of death related to the act of life?

Unless we die many voluntary deaths, we cut ourselves off from living itself. We come to misunderstand life, fear other people, break the very rhythm of living. Life, in its openness and continued vulnerability (devoid of hardness or cynicism), is marked by the scars of such deaths. They are the very signs of life.

Driving my car one day I spotted a bumper sticker that read: "DIE HARD—UCLA Bruins Fan." While I didn't wish to dampen any show of enthusiasm for a college football team, still this set me to reflection: Wouldn't it be best *not*, in fact, to die hard?

In my view, the best way to go gentle into that good night is to die a number of small deaths prior to the main event. Get used to the dynamics of such dying. Become accustomed to engaging the fact of death in useful, positive, ordinary and simple ways. Small deaths become life-affirming experiences. They concern basic, nitty-gritty matters.

What are some of the things that stand in the way of successful living? All of us know them. They include, for example, pride, despair, anger, anxiety, and envy. We are acquainted with them intimately. Small deaths can mean they no longer exert telling control over our lives. As we become free of their domination, so our lives grow fuller and richer.

Then, after a lifetime of such small deaths, we are able to approach death itself with equanimity, peace, a certain familiarity, and a sense of confidence. Let me suggest some possible small deaths. What can we do about them?

Take perfectionism. It strives to create a controlled, false world. It dislikes warts, sudden rainfall, delays, someone who has to walk slowly through a busy intersection using a cane, a child's cluttered nursery, unscheduled sex, having to take a shit at an inconvenient moment, and the acknowledgment of an embarrassing problem in a relationship. A stiff order. But when we relinquish perfectionism and quit playing god, it can be a happy occasion for fireworks, band music, and chilled wine.

Take arrogance. Some of us decide we can operate as power brokers more efficiently when we create intricate labyrinths that cause others to lose their way (and confidence), and find redemption only when we save them (and make them utterly reliant on us). Or, we construct high walls around areas at home or work, restricting the free movement of others, and allowing us closer scrutiny of them as well as tighter control. When this dismal situation is granted a merciful small death, openness can be the result. As Walt Whitman wrote in *Leaves of Grass:* "Unscrew the locks from the doors! Unscrew the doors themselves from their jambs!"

Take sloth. A small death can turn it into motivation.

Take anger. *You* take it, please! It is such a bore. People who carry resentments mar the landscape. Get *over* it! Get help. Wake up. Our days and years are numbered. Don't waste them in rage. Honor life. Treat it as holy.

Take prejudice. Battles and wars, conflagration and disasters can result from it. One moment in my memory stands out unforgettably as Exhibit A of prejudice. In the inner city of Indianapolis in 1958 I saw a small white boy jab a knife into a wooden pole on the street and recite over and over as in a mantra, "I wish it was a nigger." I never forgot the scene, its grotesqueness and deep sadness. Whatever may be our choice of prejudice, let us say "Enough!" Let it perish in a convenient small death.

Take selfishness and greed. This is when we want the whole cherry pie, the entire chocolate cake, *all* the french fries. We want the next village, that mountain over there, the state, the archipelago, a small ocean, the next continent. We want MGM, Paramount, Universal, Fox, Disney, and Miramax. All that we possess isn't sufficient; we want *yours*. A cool small death can change this to thanks for the manifold blessings of life, and sharing what we have.

Take living in the past. Norma Desmond in *Sunset Boulevard* is our best contemporary example. It isn't any fun. It wrecks a lot of lives and can be a picture of hell, as evidenced by this description from T. S. Eliot: ". . . the final desolation of solitude in the phantasmal world of imagination, shuffling memories and desires." Give yesterday the boot. Greet the new dawn. Buy a new hat. Burn some old letters. Deliberately start a new friendship.

Take subterfuge and lies. This one is dirty, but seldom do we get caught red-handed. Meanwhile, we continue to wreak havoc and play Machiavellian games with other people's lives. The telephone is a useful instrument for this, so is the Internet, the U.S. mail, and the coffee hour. Someone else's reputation can sometimes be shredded (if we're clever) in ten minutes. A small death means salvation for numberless victims.

Take indecision. My favorite example of this is found in Christopher Fry's play *The Dark Is Light Enough*. The Countess speaks of Richard, an observer caught in indecision:

> *Richard sometimes reminds me of an*
>   *unhappy*
> *Gentleman, who comes to the shore*
> *Of a January sea, heroically*
> *Strips to swim, and then seems powerless*
> *To advance or retire, either to take the shock*
> *Of the water or to immerse himself again*
> *In his warm clothes, and so stands cursing*
> *The sea, the air, the season, anything*
> *Except himself, as blue as a Plucked goose.*
> *It would be very well if he would one day*
> *Plunge, or dress himself again.*

A small death here means to quit standing naked on the shore in the cold, and *deciding* (this is the operative word) to get wet or else to dress and go home. Richard, in Fry's play, is someone we can recognize in ourselves as well as others. Richard's predicament is terribly funny, but also poignant. He is divided against himself. It can be bloody cold out there on the shore of a January sea.

Take stubbornness. Civilizations periodically perish over this one, because it gets mixed with ego and pride. "I won't, I won't, I WON'T!" Lighten up. Tell someone you're sorry. Give a blessing instead of a curse. Write a check to pay a debt. Don't grasp power as a lifeline. Dying a small death to stubbornness won't kill you. Indeed, it is good for your health in body and soul, here and in eternity.

Take anxiety. This is an itch. When it gets really bad, it resembles a brush with poison ivy. Relief is hard to come by if we refuse to change. Give it a graceful coup de grace. Practice faith, practice love, practice hope. Live in the moment freely.

Take the refusal to be grateful for what one clearly possesses. Since some of the richest people in the world are frequently guilty of this, it clearly isn't a matter of not being able to change a scene, make a purchase, change partners, seek entertainment or exert power. The solution seems to lie within oneself. A small death here apparently means a refusal to live primarily on the surface of life, being a perpetual surfer, and to seek otherworldly riches and spiritual wisdom inside the wonderful universe of one's own being. Poet Marianne Moore pointed out the riches of solitude as an antidote to loneliness. Poet May Sarton discovered a bountiful inner life in the company of seasons, friends, birds and animals, flowers and the sea. Let this small death open the way to becoming an explorer of the inner life.

Take pride. This stands arrogantly in the way of so much honest expression, so many human possibilities. We have all witnessed the tragedy that results when pride destroys a family's well-being, an organization's progress, a city's vitality, anyone's spiritual growth. Too, we have observed how pride can cause great pain in the life of an individual who is its victim. C. P. Snow in *The Masters* left us this portrait: "With him intimacy could only flow one way . . . He was so made that he could not bear the equality of the heart." A small death can change pride, soften it, open it to an acknowledgement of vulnerability and a desire to change. Love can be a strong factor here; so can moving outside pride's isolation into the mutuality of life in a community.

Pride does not always occupy a great stage. It insinuates itself in many small ways. I learned this early. In high school in the thirties, I was embarrassed when I had to face myself as an insensitive nitwit, a proud fool. My high school sponsored an annual essay writing contest. In the preceding two years I had won honorable mention. Now I was a senior, and this would be my last chance to try for first prize. I did my best, as I saw it, and submitted the essay to my teacher, Mary E. Lowe. The assigned theme of the paper was the American revolutionary war.

After reading it, Miss Lowe said, "It's good, Malcolm, but it can't win. You've written about the war, but I can't smell the sweat, can't see the blood. You haven't made it real." Only two days remained before the deadline for submitting the essay. I was determined to win. I pushed myself beyond limits, concentrated wholly on the task, kept sleep and relaxation to a minimum. Somehow I managed to write a completely new essay and meet the deadline. I told myself: I'll show *her*! *Now* she'll smell the sweat and see the blood!

I won first prize, took my bows, gratefully accepted my prize money, and even got my picture in the newspaper. But I was too proud—after all, I did it—to share the prize publicly with Miss Lowe. Yet she had surely won it with me. Without her, I would not have won. It was a

stupid, inexcusable, graceless example of poor manners—
and pride. I want to thank Miss Lowe, although it is cru-
elly late. And I realize that it is necessary for me to
continue dying many small deaths when it comes to
pride, before final leave-taking.

Take isolation. It tends to shut out other people,
new ideas, fresh energy, even the comfort of holiness,
which we're told is mysteriously linked to being in community. A character in Jean Paul Sartre's play *No Exit*
utters the classic line "Hell is—other people!" Taking a
humorous, sardonic approach to the same idea, artist
William Steig came up with his celebrated drawing of
an unhappy man seated uncomfortably inside a small,
square box. The caption read "People are no damn
good."

Almost everybody has felt this way. When I was a
young man, locked into feeling that I didn't actually
understand anyone else *or* myself, I identified with Celia
in T. S. Eliot's *The Cocktail Party,* who said:

> *"No . . . it isn't that I want to be alone,*
> *But that everyone's alone—or so it seems*
>   *to me.*

*They make noises, and think they are
      talking to each other;
They make faces, and think they under-
      stand each other.
And I'm sure that they don't. Is that a
      delusion?"*

God, this touched me deeply. I suffered a terrible feeling of aloneness at that time. It was sharply accentuated by a routine of ordinary encounters, small talk, and what seemed a choreographed existence. At its worst, it was solitary confinement. Later, although I was occupied with people—as a young priest I was surrounded by them—I had a painful sense of alienation. A part of the problem was that I hid behind my clerical collar and liturgical robes, attempting to *perform* the role of a priest as I had learned it. This intrinsically isolated me *as a person* from others. My prescribed role undercut the possibility of mutuality. So it became necessary to undergo the death of moving away from alienation. I had to find ways of relating to people, listening to them, accepting them as authentic beings, and finding (and admitting) how much I needed them in my life. By doing this, my life was transformed.

Like isolation, envy is bad for the soul. Sometimes it works like acid on our spirit. This can be all the more painful if a person whom we envy is close by. I have envied certain people from time to time, usually when my own vanity was threatened by someone else's success. This did not prepare me, though, for a genuine crisis in my life years ago when I moved in a social and professional circle with a particular group of writers and artists.

Slowly, it dawned on me that envy of one of them had become an overwhelming problem for me. The malaise sullied my nice, clean, virtuous self-portrait. This was serious stuff. It grabbed me by the short hairs. What could I do? Withdraw from the fray? Move to southern France?

This writer and I served together on several professional committees and often attended the same parties. I saw him as gifted, disciplined, productive, outgoing, and passionate about his work while also admirably self-controlled and in sure command of his talents. His sheer energy was formidable. He loomed as someone far superior to me. I could even acknowledge that he was likable, even lovable, possessing great charm.

Clearly, a small death was in order on my part. The writer had done nothing to irritate, frustrate, and disturb me other than to be himself. The fault of the envy was in me. I do not remember exactly how, or when, I discovered what I must do. I admired this person very much. Underneath my envy, I liked him. From an objective viewpoint, I appreciated him. Our lives had been thrust together by some mysterious accident of fate. Honestly and without pretense, I decided I would try to become his friend. So I spent more time with him on projects of mutual interest. Soon we hung out together, had fun, and relaxed. If there remained a seductive twinge of envy, it was finally dissipated in shared camaraderie. My small death permitted new life, for which I was grateful.

Take despair. It is close to hopelessness, the very nadir of depression. This is the moment when we have come to the conclusion that we don't deserve love, hurt innocent bystanders in life, possess no skills in a highly competitive world, are doomed to continue misusing alcohol or drugs, and/or were simply born in the wrong century. Zap. That's it. There's nothing left to say or do. Ring down the curtain.

Allowing despair to die a small death is to remove oneself from the center of the universe (a space that has God's name written on it), rejoin the human race, ask for help, accept help, refuse to surrender hope, and let the play continue. I know many stirring, inspirational, gut-wrenching, breathtakingly vivid stories of men and women who have climbed out of a snake pit or a pile of dung, come back to a full and rewarding life, and lived in joy to tell the tale. When they emerged, they somewhat resembled the mythical figure of Lazarus, at first. Like him, they wore stinking graveclothes and slowly unloosed their bindings as they grew accustomed to freedom and new life.

There was not a whit of sentimentality in their experience; it was stark, brutally realistic, severely life-threatening. However, they survived, and did so with grace. Their stories are testaments of hope. They prove to me that the unconditional love of God is present in pits of despair—radical, dynamic, forgiving, healing, and life-transforming. It points the way from here to there, providing a glimpse of eternity.

CHAPTER 4

A Quiet Place

In order to give life a chance to fulfill its possibilities, we need to make time for perspective, focusing, and reflection. It is necessary to find a quiet place and nurture an inner life. A number of ways are available to us.

One is to take seriously our dreams, understand and interpret them. My own are infinitely varied, bringing up myriad images for me. In one, I encounter a father who has kind, luminous eyes and a face bathed in light, reminiscent of a figure in a Rembrandt painting. Our meeting marks a significant return, even a homecoming, and I am overcome with feeling. In another dream, my life is quickly and radically changing. Indeed, I must catch a train that will depart shortly from a station. Happy to go, I deliberately leave behind my accumulated luggage, tightly packed suitcases, and heavy trunks. (I welcome the chance for a fresh start, a new beginning, a focus that lets me see things in a different and more positive way.)

Another dream reveals a huge, dark room. I stand directly outside it, looking through an open door. I am in a circle of bright light. I believe someone is hidden in the threatening dark space, who can see me clearly. I feel wholly vulnerable and I am afraid, yet I need to communicate with whoever is in the dark room. I ask myself: Why do I wait here in fear? Why don't I leave the bright room and walk into the dark? (I need to deal with my fears, be courageous, confront the realities of my life, take hard risks.)

It is important inner work to keep a dream journal, record dreams, explore their meanings and what they have to tell us. One dream stands out particularly in my memory. I hear someone cry out in anguish as if under torture. Awakening, I realize with a start that the man who cried out is a part of me. He yearns to communicate, move from entombment, enter freely into the warp and woof of my life, and share it. Immediately I know that I must help him, become involved with him, and let him come in. He is one of the several characters who comprise the whole cast of myself. It is his time to be on stage, read his lines, and interact with the other parts of myself.

I welcome wholeness as a substitute to my old fragmentation. There are any number of quiet places that can nourish our inner life.

For example, places of spiritual holiness. I remember with affection a rural chapel where, in the early morning, I watched the reflection of stained-glass windows behind the altar-creating a pool of color on the bare stone floor. At first I could perceive only pure blue and yellow. Then, as the sun crept higher, red began to run slowly along a sharp edge of stone. Soon it mixed with the other colors, creating a design and movement. This provided a sense of mystery and the numinous, an aid to reflection and prayer.

Once, visiting the Iona Community on an island off the coast of Scotland, I sat late at night in the restored ruins of the abbey with its ancient stones. A single candle burned on the altar. I was startled out of my personal meditation when a bat flew back and forth, casting an irregular, moving shadow. Its unrest and frenzy reminded me of the world outside, which needed to be as spiritually significant to me as my own soul.

Journeys into nature perhaps provide us with our most compelling quiet places and opportunities to nurture our inner life. I have known nature in remote parts of the U.S., Canada, Mexico, Israel and France. Some of the holiest places I've known were in forests and mountain areas. The sound of a brook or stream insinuated itself into my consciousness. I was surrounded by great trees and all kinds of animals. At nighttime I looked up and saw stars so close, I felt that I could touch them. Moments like these can be overwhelming in their spiritual power, conveying the sheer wonder of creation and its immensity, one's own intimacy with it, and a revelation of deep purpose.

Hiking, looking at a vista that combines dozens of elements including sky and hills, has offered me an awesome sense of being in the very midst of what is holy. At certain moments, when my eyes drank in more than they could understand, it seemed as if I were in death, as well as life. The intensity was nearly unbearable, yet I knew that I had to be fully in it. I thought: God is here too; I am not in this place alone. It was like an epiphany.

In luminous moments, the stark beauty of creation leaps out at us. Josephine W. Johnson caught this in *The Inland Island:* "The bloodroot leaves had grown enormous as lily pads, and at the roots of trees the fiddler ferns uncoiled, pale grey-green, dry hollow scales, and the old winter ferns still beautiful, flat as crocodiles on the ground around them." Perceiving the wonder of such creation and beauty, our focus changes from the immediate to the eternal, from chaos to form, from desperation to peace.

The inner life and the inner journey must progress simultaneously with our outer lives. Laurens Van Der Post wrote about both in *Venture to the Interior.* He described the journey a person takes inside while also embarking upon an exterior one. It's vital that we maintain a careful balance when we attempt to do this. Most of us who do not live a cloistered existence must discern spiritual meanings in every sort and condition of place.

This is why I pray the wildest variety of prayers. For example, prayer can be laced with color and fun, despair and pain, vitality and a sense of renewal. Prayer can be (in addition to words) a number of very different things: Voting. Making love. Cooking. Watering a garden. Marching in a peace demonstration. Listening. Lying on a sick bed. Dancing. Swimming. Meeting someone. Starting a job. Walking on a crowded street.

I like to look out at life as I see it, and pray about it. I pray as I drive my car on an expressway. I pray in a crowded supermarket filled with every sort of person. I pray at work during a tough staff meeting. I pray at home, sometimes in a more leisurely way, for example when I am cooking. Years ago I was terribly shocked when a friend of mine, a symphony conductor, told me he had stood at the grave of his young son and was unable to pray because he did not know the words of a prayer. He had no idea that he prayed in the very act of standing there with the intention to pray.

His story led me to discover non-verbal prayer. My favorite non-verbal prayer appeared in a workshop that I led. I asked the participants to bring a prayer to the next class. One woman brought a dance which she performed, another sang a song. A man baked an apple pie and brought it to the workshop. We ate an honest and good prayer.

I have also found prayer in scary, lonely situations when my own life seemed confronted by a brick wall that blocked my way. One day around fifteen years ago I had reached a low ebb in my life. There seemed to be no movement or anticipation or joy. Everything was at a standstill, or so I felt. Impenetrable darkness offered no possibility of light. I had unresolved needs that appeared larger and more formidable than huge stone boulders. My burdens, without peace, were unendurable.

Faced by an overwhelming need to converse with God on the most realistic terms, I walked alone on the beach. The ocean spread out to infinity before me. As always when I walk on the beach, I picked out two small stones from the surf. They had come from the ocean, from the deep. They made me feel anchored to the whole of creation when I held one in the palm of each hand.

Then I poured out my heart to God. My intention was not to use God to respond positively to a wish of mine. I was telling God there needed to be a shift in the movement of my life journey. I was open to God's answer, even if I did not want it when it came. I explained that I trusted God, so I would accept what came.

God (I said), please be God in my life now. Please let me understand that you move in my life. Somehow, please, communicate with me.

In due time, ensuing weeks and months, my prayer was answered. Not in any DeMilleian echo-chamber. It was answered quietly in my heart. My life changed, radically and completely, in positive ways that brought it fresh purpose, an anchor of love, and renewed motivation.

I had felt dead, and was brought to life again. I was without hope, and found it. I was unable to see love, but soon was surrounded by it. So I experienced a new life, chapter, opportunity, fresh opening.

This came to me after I had found a quiet place within myself where I could reflect, meditate, and pray.

The journey into self, when properly conducted, is a healing trip. It means going into deep water and underneath it. There is no way to do this except by faith. A Buddhist view is that if we can be empty enough, the divine voice can speak through us. I find this akin to Jesus' emptying himself of power and nakedly embracing humanity; filling himself with God's will, and allowing God to take over completely in his life.

To prepare for his public ministry, Jesus remained for forty days in the wilderness. "He was among the wild beasts, and the angels waited on him." The wilderness experience remains, for us, one of the best places to be spiritually. It is a place or condition of heightened awareness and stark reality, without escape clauses.

For those of us who participated actively in the civil rights movement of the sixties, the wilderness experience and our spiritual experience became one. There were times of risk and sacrifice. Some of our more difficult moments, including public confrontation, arrest and jailing, were also occasions of spiritual awakening.

In the face of hard strife, I learned the meaning of nonviolence. I saw hate close up in life-threatening situations. A friend of mine, Jonathan Daniels, perished in one of these. Another, Viola Liuzzo, was murdered in such a situation. Both deaths underscored for me the fact that prayer involves action.

While prayer is sometimes polite and formal and neat, at other times it is sweaty and earthy and desperate. Of course, prayer is not just about personal needs; it also concerns the needs of Earth, and of men, women, and children. Prayer is asked in the midst of pain for health; in the midst of agony for justice. So I found that my own prayer changed gradually from convenient personal petitions in the dark midnight of my soul to meditations and entreaties for others.

Soon I realized in the struggle for justice that it is necessary to change not only laws, but human hearts as well.

And that if we do not practice love within ourselves—including loving self in a healthy way—we cannot help to bring about social change, and even stand in the way of it. I learned painfully that one generation cannot completely solve great problems. Each new generation must be prepared to struggle with them in imaginative, fresh, courageous, and faithful ways.

A Buddhist teaching is that the spiritual answer is not to renounce the world, but to work for change within the world where inner strengths will be tested. Similarly, my Christian faith was relevant one day in the early sixties in Atlanta when I was part of a sit-in at a downtown department store that segregated against African Americans.

After we had been rounded up by the police, we were placed in a large elevator on an upper floor. An African American woman was its operator. As the elevator slowly made its descent, we quietly sang "We Shall Overcome." A few occupants stared at us in undisguised hatred. Others, including the elevator operator, wept quietly. We were making our simple witness, and also paying the price for it. We were practicing nonviolence. This meant accepting the consequences of our action.

We were eons away from a comfortable, safe, isolated existence; from the respectability and prestige of organized religion; from social acceptance. However, I believe Christ was in the wilderness with us.

In this same vein, I see Martin Luther King, Jr.'s, *Letter from the Birmingham Jail* as an epistle from the wilderness and his best piece of writing. Earlier, from Nazi Germany, came martyr Dietrich Bonhoeffer's *Letters and Papers from Prison.* Later, Breyton Breytenbach wrote about his wilderness experience during seven years in a South African prison, when he was once in complete isolation for two years.

It is ironic that the wilderness experience provides a quickening of the spirit, while much safe, privileged religion is like a Muzak-softened space and time that only provides comfort and easy listening. Where is meaning? In the wilderness, when our souls are dry and parched, we are enabled to cry out in the passion of deep caring and intense involvement. This stems from having found, and spent some time in, a quiet place as an inner soulful experience.

The Trappist monk and author Thomas Merton addressed the world from a quiet place, the Abbey of

Gethsemani in Kentucky. I remember a day in the sixties when I trudged up a muddy path to his hermitage. We spent the afternoon together. He astonished me; he lived as a hermit, yet had the new Bob Dylan album and (it seemed) all the most recent books. He was deeply involved in the life of the world, while not physically active in it. We discussed subject after subject in a torrent of conversation—war, race, spirituality, literature—knowing our time together was short. We gossiped. He served me Kentucky bourbon, which we sipped slowly.

The one flaw in his experience, he explained, was that he could not see films or plays because he lived an isolated rural life and was not allowed to spend his time outside the abbey. (Yet he still included French film director Jean-Luc Godard in our conversation.) Humor, easy grace, and gentle openness marked his warm adventure of involvement in all of life.

Merton wisely included play, relaxation, fun, and humor in his overall spirituality. I suggest that on our own spiritual journey we include these. Use our imaginations. Walk up a road we have long wondered or dreamt about. Study its detail. Discern a house, a tree, a lamppost, a dog, a car. Be aware of shadows, colors, patterns.

This can aid our perspective and focus, which are essential for spiritual survival. Discover the mixed definitions of beauty in the world. Look for eternal meanings.

As a child growing up, I always had certain secret gardens that were places of inner nurturing and involved my imagination (I suspect that you did, too). My earliest one was in Central Park in the heart of New York City. I climbed rocks leading to the fortress or the castle. Adults knew it as the park observatory. However, I wasn't fooled for a moment. I knew it was the unapproachable fortress (except for me), the mysterious castle surrounded by a moat (but I had access to it).

Later, during my urban childhood's year-long visit to rural Texas, I explored dry gulleys outside Rockdale. Nearby, fields of bluebonnets and Indian blanket flowers blossomed. Below, in dirt labyrinths made by the gulley, I discovered—yes!—the crater of the moon.

My favorite secret garden was in Colorado Springs, Colorado, where I attended junior high school. It was surrounded by a wooden fence in such disrepair that it seemed about to fall down. Inside were weeds and wild flowers growing tall, and an ancient tree that was my link to a primeval, primordial Druid rite under a full moon long ago. Curiously, it also reminded me of Sherwood Forest where Robin Hood and I had played and worked . . .

I believed firmly that I was the only person who had ever entered that secret garden. Propping myself against the trunk of the friendly tree, I lay secure on the soft ground. There was such extraordinary peace here. I ached with pain when the time came for me to depart. I walked outside the worn wooden gate, looking back with sharp joy, bearing within myself the recognition of absolutely *belonging* somewhere. It seemed an outpost of heaven, a place in eternity that was entirely mine; at least it was a piece of Earth that welcomed me unconditionally, gave me a haven, and bestowed a sense of peace I found nowhere else.

Even now, I have my secret gardens. A few are on patches of land beneath the sun and moon. Others exist only in the recesses of my imagination, thoughts, and memories. I need them when life becomes too fast and demanding, and resembles a locomotive racing along a track without anyone driving it. Then I call a halt, claim a time of silence and peace, start slowly again with a fresh perspective.

I speak to God: "I don't hide from you or seek to. What would be the point? You see every part of me. You fill not only the present and eternity, but all of life's fragments, cracks, splinters, openings, and fractures. With you, I find communion instead of loneliness. I cherish being with you in a secret garden, a wilderness, and a quiet place." I seek healing, quietness, joy, and peace. I need this link between my personal spiritual life, on the one hand, and the big picture of public spirituality and religion, on the other. I must have contemplation as well as activity.

Quiet. One hand clapping in the forest. Listening. Waiting. Waiting upon God. Not being the initiator, but allowing God to initiate. This is hard for those who always have an agenda to push with God. Dorothy L. Sayers wrote a great play, *The Zeal of Thy House,* that concerns one person's refusal to surrender to God and insistence on playing God. The person comes to a moment of truth and salvation. Yet the truth is that in order to offer our energy to God, we need to bring it down, and make it a free gift.

As adults, we need the childlike experience of secret gardens. Without them, we might lose humor, sanity, and grace—and our awareness of the child within each of us. Writer Paul Elmen described the Christian life as having a Pickwickian sense of the queerness and joy of living, its endless novelty, quiet rhythms, and soaring flights. The point is: We cannot see with our human eyes all there is to see. We need to see mystery and faith, hope and love. To become absorbed in the small rhythms and awesome mysteries of life requires spiritual energy. This, in turn, requires commitment and discipline. These words aren't exactly fashionable. Discipline is often unpleasant, but can yield a peaceful harvest of life.

The stress of life is dizzying, impersonal, and harsh. We have need of a place to rejuvenate, catch our breath, become enabled to go on. This is why a quiet place is essential. I recall how writer Nathanael West said Hollywood is not so much a place as a state of mind. This is also true of our secret gardens and some of our quiet places.

As we pass through our earthly life, we're giving, taking, experiencing, sharing, loving, and struggling. We are here on a visa, for this is not our permanent home. Finding a quiet place can remind us that, after we die, we will come home to where our passport is valid.

Many of us have learned how to share our secret gardens and quiet places with other people. They have shared theirs with us, too. We recognize a mutual dependence on having an inner life to sustain us at times of stress, anxiety, danger, and crisis. So we have reached out to one another, giving and receiving help. We know the deepest meaning of life is not to be found in a solitary search for bliss, but in unselfish involvement with others—and with the environment, the call of justice, and the primacy of love.

On the basis of this, I believe that in eternity we shall be confronted by the challenge of creative growth with far greater intensity than even at this present time. We shall continue our spiritual journey with full impetus. What, then, of peace?

Peace carries vastly different meanings. One is comfort and passivity. Another, addressed by theologian Karl Barth, acknowledges there is a sinking and suffering, a being lost and being rent asunder in the peace of God. A great hymn also catches this same theme: "Contented, peaceful fishermen, before they ever knew the peace of God that filled their hearts brimful, and broke them too . . . The peace of God, it is no peace, but strife closed in the sod."

It seems that karma is a major force of our lives. We need to learn in *this* life forgiveness, tenderness, healing, sharing, compassion, and loving. A simplistic and rather stupid picture is presented when eternal life with God is seen as a timeless, idyllic picnic below a heavenly waterfall, or an extension of Disneyland. It is far, far more significant than that, with a deeper and soberer purpose. It is also far more hopeful, realistic, and life-affirming.

For we are engaged upon a life journey, a pilgrimage, a splendid adventure of the soul with God. God loves us. Peace with God means growth, spiritual development, adhering to ways that bring our humanity into focus and enhance it, and having hope and confidence in an eternal life that is solidly built on what happens to us in this one. If we understand this and act on it, it can guide us when the time comes for us to go into that good night.

CHAPTER 5

Cultivate Simplicity

We are not permanent here. We're passing through. Certainly we'll take nothing with us.

I wonder how Alexander the Great dealt with this. It must have been hard for him, having conquered the world. Emperors notoriously place power ahead of goodness, strength ahead of mercy.

If we own possessions here, we leave them here. Pharaohs seemed assured they could take their treasures with them into eternity. They were buried with food and drink, jewels and wealth. Fools. We brought nothing into this world and we will take nothing out of it.

I was shown a poignant example of this one day when I was asked to visit the apartment of a woman who had died in order to water her plants. After I let myself in, I found a space quiet as a tomb with the exception of the heavy tick-tock of a huge grandfather clock in the hall. Everything was in place—chairs, tables, plants, books, pictures, a stove, a frig. Only she wasn't. Her mail had piled up. I realized with a start that the mail doesn't stop when we die. It was all to be forwarded to her brother in Kansas City.

Wandering from room to room, I observed fragments of her life: A piece of jewelry, a magazine opened to a page, a quiet electric clock in her bedroom that marked passing moments. I watered the plants. The frig had been turned off, so when I opened its door I found rotten food, which I placed in a garbage bag.

Standing in the hall, I wondered if the woman who had lived here might simply walk in unexpectedly, as actress Gene Tierney did in the movie *Laura*. What if the announcement of her death was premature? When she came through the door would she look puzzled at my presence and then indignantly demand to know what I was doing here?

Departing, I turned the key in the lock of the front door. I was terribly aware that the woman who had rented the apartment took nothing with her. And I suddenly was overcome by a sense of the futility of many possessions and the irony that all must be left behind when we depart.

I remember one afternoon when a woman came to see me for counseling. She was fifty, African-American, the wife of a prominent businessman. She drove an expensive car, shopped and used a brace of credit cards, and she had come to see me to talk about meaning.

It had more or less vanished from her life. Her children were grown and had departed to work out their own destinies. Her husband was a workaholic, away from early morning until late in the evenings making a great deal of money. She felt lonely and adrift, unable to find any real meaning in her existence. I told her she could easily look forward to thirty or more years and that she needed to go back to school or get a part-time job or start serious volunteer work. Her whole future hung in the balance.

The other day I had lunch with a highly successful young executive in the music business. He was thirty-something, charming, and intelligent. His future appeared unlimited in terms of making money and accumulating power. But over lunch he seemed distressed, restless, and agonized because he felt unfulfilled. Already he had serious health problems; stress was an arch-enemy knocking at the gate. He said he had no time for love or cultivating a relationship. I asked if he took time for reflection.

"I don't have any time for reflection now," he said, looking at me with a sad smile. "I've just got to make it. Maybe I can reflect later."

It occurred to me I was lunching with the equivalent of the rich young ruler in the gospel who, although drawn to Jesus, avoided commitment and pensively withdrew. The executive needed to ask deep questions about meaning: "Who am I? Where am I going? Why? Do I want to go there? If not, where do I want to go? Why? What am I even doing here at this moment?"

Yet he shelved the questions and avoided wondering where the responses might lead. No time to find out. No time for reflection.

I think there *are* ghosts. They include people who, while they accumulated symbols of achievement, never found an inner life. They never actually learned how to let go and experience honest relationships, mutuality, vulnerability, and understanding. So, after death, these ghosts continue to roam through homes they occupied, spaces they filled, crying out in their incompleteness and eternal restlessness.

In Hollywood during the forties I knew some such future ghosts quite intimately. I worked in the motion picture industry with legendary stars and highly motivated studio personnel, rubbed elbows at social events with many more. Dubbed "Hollywood's golden boy" by society columnist Cobina Wright, I enjoyed cocktails with Adele Astaire, tea with Lillian Gish. I was on the dance floor of Hollywood's Mocambo with Lana Turner and Ava Gardner. In New York I had brunch with Mrs. William Randolph Hearst, dinner in Beverly Hills with Marion Davies.

In my twenties, I found this exhilarating. Yet I was also quickly bored. I was working hard as well as playing hard. The Empress of Hollywood, Mary Pickford, was my business partner, mentor, and friend. She reigned in her estate, Pickfair, which was almost as well-known as the White House. I learned to swim in its kidney-shaped pool, and dined there often. Mary introduced me to her friends.

At parties I mingled with Judy Garland, Joan Crawford, Cary Grant, Myrna Loy, John Wayne, Ingrid

Bergman, Gary Cooper, Elizabeth Taylor, Clark Gable, Judith Anderson, and many more. I saw them only as highly interesting people who were employed in the same industry as I was. Now when I rent videos of their old movies, I realize they have inadvertently become this century's gods and goddesses. But they seemed totally mortal to me then!

Charlie Chaplin, Jr., the son of the great actor, and I were friends. One New Year's Eve he and I were night-clubbing on the Sunset Strip. Charlie drove a new black Cadillac given him for Christmas by his father. We had departed Ciro's and were headed for the Mocambo when Charlie's car collided with another. Within moments the police were there. It must have been a dull New Year's Eve from a news standpoint because, the next morning, our minor auto accident was emblazoned in banner headlines on all the front pages.

Later that morning Charlie and I went to his father's house, located a couple of blocks from Pickfair. We breakfasted with Mr. Chaplin, who wore an elegant suit and tie, and appeared distraught and distant. I understood that he felt persecuted by the media, alienated from the American public because of bad publicity.

Shortly afterward, he left the U.S. to live in Switzerland. For all his fame and wealth, he was devoid of inner peace.

Mine was a rich life with a great cast of characters and endless glamour. But soon I grew disenchanted. When I grew older I didn't want to be like the highly successful men and women who now surrounded me. Many misused alcohol and other drugs; others had the most tragic relationships and unhappy personal lives. Apparently they lived and died for what they called success. In my view their careers were empty charades, their lives agonizingly self-destructive. Why live that way?

So I came to a growing realization that I wanted something quite different. It could be identified as meaning, or a different journey, even a deliberate search for truth and simplicity. After much reflection and immersion in scripture and prayer, I felt called to become a priest.

Entering an Episcopal seminary to pursue a theological education in 1951, I had commenced a spiritual odyssey that would take me in directions I had never dreamed of. While simplicity would prove to be elusive for many years to come, at least I had opted for it.

By simplicity I do not mean the absence of struggle and conflict. Instead I refer to the task of defining and working with basics. Sometimes we can be moving so furiously that our shadow itself seems to do a dance. I had been like that in my driven Hollywood years—rootless, responding to life as if it were an electric current. I had avoided being conscious of the present moment because of my absorption in the future. I had run away from intimacy.

I ultimately found it's foolish, however, to sell one's soul for a few lousy bucks or fifteen seconds of fame.

This reminds me of a true story told me by a renowned American writer about another man whom he considered one of the most promising young poets to appear in decades on the literary scene. The poet's work, he felt, was original, incisive, absolutely beautiful. One day the poet shocked his New York friends, including the writer, when he announced he was leaving to take a job as a writer in a movie studio in Hollywood.

"How can you do that?" the seasoned writer asked the young poet. "What will happen to your poetry?"

"Don't worry," the poet replied. "My wife and I are going to live in a cheap apartment. We'll drive a used

VW. We're putting the money away so we can move to Italy in a year or so. Then I'll write my poetry."

After the poet moved and took the job, the writer did not hear from him. However, a couple of years later the writer paid a visit to Hollywood. Outside a major studio he was nearly run down by a large convertible.

"Hi," said the poet, ensconced in the driver's seat. "Come up to the house for lunch."

The poet drove the writer to his mansion atop a hill. The poet's wife had a matching convertible. The house had a pool and tennis court. The poet did not mention Italy. The poet did not mention poetry. The poet was not a poet anymore.

How can we hold onto basics, fundamental ideas and ideals in our lives? Avoid being sold to the highest bidder? Cultivate simplicity? I learned valuable lessons about this when I journeyed to a remote village in rural France in 1957 to spend a few months in the Taizé monastic community. I was there for the public ritual of the life profession of Brother Mark in September of that year.

Certain highly reassuring and spiritually significant words were used in the service.

March. There was a sense of strong, decisive, purposive movement. Do not dawdle; time is of the essence, and it is precious.

Abandon yourself. Here was a sense of losing oneself in the greater purpose of God. Giving to other people quite genuinely in order to meet their needs and to offer support. This includes helping them to work through self-constructed barriers. Finally, you may be able to offer them the gift of discerning beauty, value, and dignity in themselves—especially if they do not.

Renouncing to look back. Live in the present. Do not romanticize or sentimentalize the past. Do not let the present escape you.

Joyful. Choose to live joyfully now. Live joyfully with what we have now. Live joyfully with the others who are present now. Try to avoid being obsessed by frustration, anxiety, and stress.

Thankfulness. Most of us have had experiences of being unhappy or unfulfilled, being treated as victims, or oppressed. So, our thankfulness for what we have can be wonderfully real, even rather startling in a world where saying thanks is often put away with mothballs.

Simplify your life. Reject useless burdens in order to help carry those of others. To live in mercy means self-forgetfulness. The rule of Taizé says that the spirit of perfection is wrong when it is seen as imposing our own point of view as the best.

There are specific things we can do to focus on simplicity in our life. I like this Tibetan Buddhist saying:

> *Do you have the patience to wait*
> *till your mud settles and the water is clear?*
> *Can you remain unmoving*
> *till the right action arises by itself?*

This affords a wise correction for activism that is devoid of spiritual vision and is ego-centered, sporadic, and leads nowhere. It requires patience, a quiet strategy, a decision to work with others in community instead of tilting at windmills. It allows God to be a part of the action. It is worth all the effort to find a needed balance.

One of my favorite books is Walter M. Miller's *A Canticle for Leibowitz,* offering a glimpse into a future where structures of society have been shattered by devastating wars. A spiritual community located in a desert strives to preserve devotion and learning. It dedicates itself to reflection, awareness, purpose, meaning, and simplicity.

We neglect this at our peril. The practice of simplicity can take different forms. Discover the whole world of nature around you, and find your own place in it. Listen to music, write a poem, cook a marvelous dish, reflect quietly before a fire, walk in the rain, spend significant time with a friend.

I try to set up a prioritizing grid in my mind: What is most important, significant, necessary, and vital in my life? I make a list.

It can include family, faith, sex, relationships, work, leisure, justice causes, goals, desires, wishes, demands on my time, organizations to which I belong, ideals, areas of volunteerism, and also pressing matters that weigh heavily on my mind.

It is a jungle of a list. If I do not attempt to simplify it, the weight of it can crush me. Then I set out to decide what is number one, number two, number three, and what follows.

I cannot bring equal attention, wisdom, energy or commitment to each. If I try, I'll fail.

Given my understanding of self, coupled with my experience of living and what I actually believe, I gradually determine the order of the list.

Here is number one.

Here is number two.

Here is number three.

These will require my best and deepest commitment. I have decided to honor these in my mind, my heart, and my soul.

The next three or four will be dominant in the orbit of my life, but will receive somewhat less energy and devotion.

Matters that follow will necessarily be of lesser significance in the way I live my life and do what I do.

I find a workable peace in this pattern. Obviously I need to reexamine the list regularly and make changes if necessary. I try to do the best that I can with the resources given me. I accept fully (and even gratefully) my lack of perfection. I try to grow and learn, stay open to what is threatening or simply incredible, follow the dictates of my faith and conscience, honor the holiness in all persons, and work my butt off for the sake of the part of Earth that I can see and feel.

I don't try to balance the budget, distribute the wealth equally, singlehandedly save the environment, or personally usher in the realm of God.

Therefore, I am not indispensable. The world is not carried on my shoulders. I am not the Messiah, I am simply a guy by the name of Malcolm.

By setting up workable priorities that seem within the realm of possibility, while holding onto my vision of truth and justice, I try to cultivate simplicity as a significant way to set my house in order and prepare for eternity. In other words, to live fully now *and* hopefully to live fully in the life that follows.

CHAPTER 6

Free to Live, Free to Die

It matters that we tackle our foremost life problems now, grow in maturity, make strong decisions, and pay extraordinary attention to our relationships. Then we will have that particular work behind us when we move beyond death.

I believe one of the most fundamental ways we can live this life well, and prepare for eternity, is to be as open and honest as possible. Deception is bad for the soul.

We all know how a small lie can become a big one. A casual, seemingly light or relatively unimportant impersonation may turn into a long-playing role. The truth casually left unsaid on a single occasion often turns into a numbing masquerade.

When untruth is institutionalized, everybody is affected. A story is told of how Austrian Emperor Franz Joseph participated in a Maundy Thursday observance of the ritual of the "foot washing." He needed to find freedom from a paralyzing hypocrisy that enveloped his court. The feet of a dozen of the city's beggars were to be washed by the emperor. The event itself is based on Jesus' washing the feet of his disciples. Twelve of Vienna's poorest men were seated on a bench, surrounded by royal courtiers in splendid uniforms.

But the beggars' feet had already been washed and perfumed to remove any offensive odor. Years later, Consuelo Vanderbilt Balsan recalled in her memoir *The Glitter and the Gold* how cold disillusionment shone in the emperor's eyes as he beheld a ritual that had been stripped of any spiritual meaning.

Whenever highly publicized political, religious or social events and rituals are seen as pure hypocrisy, all of us are somehow betrayed. Cynicism flourishes. We ask: What can we believe in?

Writ smaller, the same kind of sham and duplicity can tear apart families and relationships, play havoc in workplaces, and dismember communities. How can we manage to be honest, tell the truth, and refuse to live a lie? In a world of shadows and labyrinths, how can we survive if we choose to be open and vulnerable?

A few committed men and women have shown us the way. To find freedom in life itself by honoring ideals, refusing to compromise, and linking personal freedom to a public declaration of liberation.

One is Dorothy Day, co-founder of the Catholic Worker movement. I remember knowing her in the late fifties. She was plain and blunt, wore simplicity like a garment, and cared passionately about justice. I found not a trace of sentimentality or banal piosity in her. She was a prophet who believed a particular truth: If you followed Christ, you sheltered the homeless and fed the hungry. Period. She said she could "feel like a failure" because "Christ was the world's greatest failure" when he died on a cross like a criminal. She comforted the afflicted and afflicted the comfortable.

Another is Martin Luther King, Jr., who observed that people hate because they fear; they fear because they do not know one another; they do not know one another because they cannot communicate; they cannot communicate because they are separated. I remember an afternoon in Selma, Alabama, when several civil rights workers followed one another into the pulpit of Brown Chapel to address a small group gathered there. When King walked in, he was tired, dusty, and sweaty. But he told us he would never make a butchery of his conscience. In other words, he would remain honest. He said what he had to say without artifice or contrived charisma. I was with him on another occasion near the end of his life. It was in Washington D.C. He had been widely criticized for his opposition to the Vietnam war; his weariness and fatigue were evident. Yet an old fire burned in his soul. Over the years, and through thick and thin, I noted how he stayed committed to his belief in justice. I recognized that this involved discipline and work, taking abuse, a connection with God and other people, and a vision.

Such passionate idealism presently seems something of an anachronism. This is sad because we need it now more than ever. Our earthly situation is fraught with dangers. In fact, the Age of Anxiety has apparently given way in part to a new, more threatening Age of Pessimism. Imaginary projections of life in the future range from the bleak to the dehumanizing.

Urban life ahead is increasingly seen in the image of the classic film *Blade Runner:* A technological jungle gone awry, with a ruined environment and a savage society. Then there are fantasies of life from outer space impinging on our own. These include aliens who attack, as well as a comet from hell that threatens the Earth's destruction.

The common denominator of the Age of Pessimism is fear, not so much of the unknown, but the known. Will we have enough money to exist and support a family's needs? If we live too long, will we find we have Alzheimer's? Will we be warehoused in impersonal nursing facilities? If we're young, have we got any chance at all? Will city streets be a battleground of violence? Are some of us doomed to exist in an underclass, without opportunity to succeed? Will an education be the earmark of the privileged? Will racism, sexism, and homophobia be exploited by demagogues who cynically use politics merely as a lever of power? Will the environment prove to be a deathly trap? If the world's population increases, will human life be impossible?

In the words of Franklin Delano Roosevelt, we need freedom from fear itself. Probably the greatest fear remains that of death or dying. Some unfortunate men and women fixate on it, suffering untold agonies for years. What is it they fear? The absence of control? The absoluteness of an end?

"To most people, death remains a hidden secret, as eroticized as it is feared," Sherwin B. Nuland observed in *How We Die.* "We are irresistibly attracted by the very anxieties we find most terrifying: We are drawn to them by a primitive excitement that arises from flirtation with danger. Moths and flames, mankind and death—there is little difference."

The worst way to die is to fear dying. We can bitterly resist it, allowing many of our fears to come together in an ultimate nightmare. Or we can try to confront our most formidable fears, including this one, in thoughtful, creative, purposive ways.

What is fear anyhow? I have found it can be elusive and mysterious, or as abrupt as a sledgehammer with deadly precision. We fear all sorts of things—spiders, God, space, the number thirteen, sex, a black cat, hell, a friendly but formidable looking St. Bernard, speed, height, water, snakes (of course), the dark, empty houses, and people in authority.

Fear can seem to be highly rational. We all know that a high-wire performer should not be afraid of height or falling. Someone delivering the mail better not be afraid of dogs. However, there are also irrational fears. For example, a world renowned entertainment star, a public idol, confided in me that her most basic fear was of success. The more adulation she received, the more her celebrity increased, the more it simply deepened her agony. "Success," she explained, "is like being on top of a flagpole. The height is dizzying. People far below resemble ants. It's cold. The wind howls. The pole is greased. I have to fight other people trying to come up and dislodge me. Enemies hurl mud and rocks at me."

Speaking personally, I am no more immune from fears than anyone else. Mine include dining alone in a restaurant, being confronted by an irrationally angry, abusive and hysterical person, and falling from a great height; a raging fire, an automobile accident, and a snake pit. But all my life I have tried to find freedom from fears.

When I was young I could not stand up in front of people and speak. When I tried, my whole body shook and I broke out in a sweat. In my early twenties I went to work for an advertising agency. I needed to make presentations to clients. What could I do? I solicited speaking engagements from advertising clubs in outlying areas where I knew no one. I shook and sweated as usual, but lost my fear. Soon I enjoyed it: The warm-up, a bit of humor, hitting my stride, getting my point across, and a strong finish. Years later I was invited to speak on many university campuses as a well-known author and activist. And I delivered hundreds of sermons as an Episcopal priest. I thoroughly enjoyed these experiences. Now I relish public speaking and the wonder of communication.

Whenever I found that fear exercised too much control over my life and even threatened my well being, I realized that my soul suffered as much as my body or mind. Was I so weak that I must permanently remain a victim? If so, what did this indicate about my spiritual progress as a human being? If I couldn't make it on Earth, how would I possibly manage in eternity?

My earliest fear was of the dark. When I was five, my parents went away for a day. They asked a neighbor to stay in the house with me. I recall that she did not like children (she certainly didn't like me) and apparently had a strong need to exert authority. I did something—I can't remember what— that upset her. She struck me on the side of my head and announced she was going to lock me inside a dark closet next to the kitchen. It held canned goods and utensils and, she said, a huge rat that would eat me.

She forced me into the closet and locked the door. The inside was cavernous and pitch-black. I screamed in utter terror, waiting for the rat to attack me. My sense of helplessness in that closet would return in nightmares for years. I pleaded through the locked door for release, beating my small fists on the hard wood to no avail. I was hysterical. I felt unloved, betrayed, at the mercy of a monster. Afterwards, I was always terrified of the dark. For years I would let a light burn at night in the next room, and crack a door open. I found it excruciatingly difficult to be on a dark street, in a dark corridor, or in an outdoor space on a dark night.

After many years of suffering from this troubling fear, I felt a strong desire to overcome it. Friends were planning to travel for a month. They lived in a rural area in a large, isolated home set back from a road amid tall trees. Would I care to house-sit? I said yes.

Now I became determined to face the fear and leave it behind. So I did not turn on the lights when darkness fell. I started to walk slowly through the rooms in the dark, feeling my way. Then I deliberately climbed up into the attic in the dark (this was a form of torture), then down wooden steps into the musty basement.

Frankensteins and jungle-fresh pythons seemed to lurk just beyond my footsteps. My heart pounded. I could scarcely breathe. Gradually however, my fear subsided. I grew accustomed to the dark and even comfortable in it. Soon, I felt supremely grateful. A scourge in my life had been removed. Now I wander easily through dark spaces without apprehension. In the darkness I can find a kind of mystery and beauty that gives me warmth and support.

Another lingering fear emerged in my youth. An angry, unleashed dog attacked and bit me one day at the beach. I remember its bared teeth, an image of terror, and the thrusting weight of its body against mine.

After that I was always terrified of dogs. During high school I sold magazines door-to-door in a city neighborhood. It was dreadful when a dog barked or, worse, appeared. When I visited friends, if a dog, tail wagging, approached me in a friendly way, my terror knew no bounds. I felt helpless.

In my thirties, when I was a graduate student, I visited Turkey. One day I was on a remote island in the bay outside Istanbul. Separated from my companions, I found myself alone on a tip of the island when I became aware suddenly of a pack of wild dogs standing on a hillside above me. The animals, closely observing my alien presence, were momentarily frozen in place. They seemed poised in formation, ready to charge down the hill and (in my imagination) tear me to pieces. I was defenseless. Instinctively, I knew I must betray no emotion, show no fear.

Somehow I held in check my thoughts and my breathing. Carefully I shifted my attention from the dogs to clouds in the sky. I walked slowly, very slowly, away from the dogs. Concentrating on lightness and easiness, I did not merely act nonchalant. I became so. The dogs did not follow me. Apparently I had become part of the landscape for them. After that, I never feared dogs again. I realized that the dogs had not caused me any trouble. Then, why fear them? Since that time I have owned and loved several dogs. Dogs are among my favorite inhabitants of the universe.

A far, far greater and more pervasive fear, a huge and awesome shadow, dominated my life for many years. It threatened my own freedom to be myself. I held it in close and unhappy isolation. It affected all of my relationships, and forced me to live with the unending stress of performing a seemingly eternal role in a script that was a cause of pain. I resided in a claustrophobic and stultifying closet labeled homosexual. Could I get free?

It was in 1976 when I became convinced the time had come for me to step outside the closet, accept the fact that I was a gay man, and get on with my life. For as far back as I could remember, I had known I was somehow different. But how? What did it mean? As a gay boy growing up, I intuited what homosexuality meant. Like virtually everyone else, I feared and disliked it. In the eyes of society it meant alien, subversive of basic values, dirty, unacceptable. In the eyes of the church, sinful. There was an absence of role models: athletes, entertainers who were out, political figures, journalists, religious leaders, teachers. Now the subject of homosexuality is on the front page and on TV. Then it was not mentioned in polite society. Gradually it dawned on me that it meant leper. Who would want to be a leper? I didn't.

I felt it was necessary to live a lie. Most of my life was a long run masquerade. Because I couldn't accept or love myself, my self-esteem was on the lowest rung. As my awareness of being gay grew, my emotions became ever more conflicted. How to live a life? I believed in the importance of honesty, yet could not be honest myself. I fought for the freedom of others (as in the civil rights movement), yet could not apparently find freedom myself. So I kept very busy, quite deliberately, in order to avoid dealing with this central issue of my life.

Finally, as a man who was deeply involved with God and other people, I felt compelled to share my truth. I desperately wished to explore life on honest terms. It seemed a moral obligation as well as a call to freedom. I knew I was created in God's own image. I knew Jesus Christ loved me unconditionally. So, what was I waiting for? Yet I had to confront fears. Given my shyness, how would I be able to handle an outburst of criticism? At fifty, what might it feel like to start over from scratch? For example, could I continue to serve as a priest?

Making my announcement, I felt like a lobster thrust into boiling water. Inevitably it was a big news story, one that would clearly alter the remainder of my life. My feelings were mixed. On the one hand, I felt a sense of exultation coming out of a locked, dark cell; and I felt confronted by infinite human possibilities. However, I also felt pain in the rejection I suffered from a number of people whom I had considered friends. I healed, adjusted, and moved into a new life.

What if I hadn't chosen to act in this freeing way, taken the risk, discarded rigidity, and embraced life? I dread to think that I could have spent the rest of my life living a lie. Freedom is a meaningless abstraction unless we honor it, love it, exercise it, respect it in the struggles of others, and personally make it our own.

Before coming out, I had known a bit of fame. In the late sixties I resided in Calhoun College at Yale as a guest fellow. One noon I was seated at lunch with students. A visitor asked me, "What do you do?" Before I could reply, a student said "He's a celebrity." At the time I was a best-selling author, frequently in the media (including *Life, Look, Time,* and *Newsweek*), interviews with Barbara Walters, David Frost, Hugh Downs, Phil Donahue, and others.

However, I had felt a growing restlessness with what seemed to be a demanding, limiting role I was expected to play. For example, I should be willing to be "on" at all times (and never deviate from a prescribed script and persona). At the same time I felt a strong need for freedom in order to find out who I was—and to be myself. I was reminded of what Philip Larkin, the English author who declined to be poet laureate of Britain, said: "I don't want to go around pretending to be me."

As I write this, twenty years later, my life's journey has brought me to rich fulfillment. I have related my faith more directly, even radically, to my life than earlier seemed possible. My faith is real to me. So is a life of service. Happily, I no longer have to rehearse a public reaction to everything in terms of image requirements; it is a splendid gift simply to abe able to be myself. I do not have to worry about deviating from a role, because there is no role.

Perhaps most significant are the fifteen years I served in a parish church in California. It proved to be a remarkable spiritual community. Since most people there were content to be themselves, I could be myself. I love preaching, and find the sermon a neglected art form. I love functioning at the altar in the eucharist.

I celebrate freedom. This includes sharing life with my beloved longtime companion of thirteen years, Mark Thompson. Although I am involved in numerous activities, ranging from AIDS chaplaincy, counseling, and teaching workshops to public speaking, I enjoy an essentially quiet existence. I water flowers and take out the garbage. I meditate and read. I go to my office and participate in a work community.

It is increasingly clear my time on Earth is limited. I anticipate death without fear. I find that I am exuberantly grateful for life. Grateful! For everything. This is freedom.

CHAPTER 7

Give Up Control

Human nature does not change. Many people make resolutions, only to break them. Make commitments, dishonoring at least some. Make promises they do not keep. What's going on here? What's the matter with us?

The answer is that we are invariably looking out for Number One. Me. Not a loved one, or neighbor, or friend, or even God. The self as deity is a contradiction in terms, and it just doesn't work. Some people try to play it all the way to the deathbed.

Deathbed confessions used to be a dandy way of dealing with the matter quite cynically. You see, some people refused to change whatsoever. They resolutely stayed cemented in position Number One until just before their demise. This required extraordinary timing.

Then, literally on their deathbed itself, they choreographed their confession. They did a magic thing. From their point of view, they were not only forgiven, but also handed a stamped passport to heaven. Just like that. Presumably as they expired they heard the sounds of a heavenly chorus bursting into song with the Hallelujah Chorus.

I believe that in order to go gentle into that good night, we need to relinquish self-sovereignty, let go, trust, and wait in a relaxed way to see what is going to happen next.

A friend of mine took rather extraordinary measures to make the switch between this world and the next. Seven months before he died of AIDS, Richard asked me to join him inside a chapel to administer the last rites.

He removed his shoes, socks and shirt, and asked me to anoint with oil the soles of his feet, his chest, and the palms of his hands. "Depart, o Christian soul, out of this world," I read. "Into your hands, o merciful Savior, we commend your servant Richard."

Richard had decided to deal fully with death then, seven months before his departure from this life. He did it in order to feel free to live the remainder of his life in the freedom and fulfillment of resurrection from the dead.

But I remember someone else who tried to hold onto life here and now, in a poignant and hopeless way. An important magazine columnist, she and I had long been acquaintances. We met unexpectedly at a big Christmas party hosted by the magazine. Sipping a Scotch, she casually told me she was terminally ill.

"But I wanted my loot," she said, referring to the obligatory holiday gifts that were her seasonal due as a person of influence. "My car trunk is full. I got all my Christmas presents—booze, books, some pieces of jewelry. My car is packed. Right after this party, I'm driving away. Going to my sister's in the country. I may be dead in three weeks. But honey, I got the loot."

The two of us stood there in the midst of the noisy party and laughed. It was a touching moment. It was also a funny, terribly real, slightly crazy one. And the laughter eased our pain.

I have found that death is not only an individual matter. Sometimes it takes on a social dimension. Albert Camus described such a situation in his novel *The Plague.*

A city is ridden by rats and the entire population is dismayed and frightened. A hotel manager lacks any understanding of his solidarity with other people. He cannot accept the reality of the awful situation and how he is just like everybody else confronted by disaster.

Death reveals a public side of itself in war, terrorism, and social upheaval. I witnessed this in Los Angeles in 1992, when riots over the Rodney King beating verdict gave rise to an unprecedented urban outbreak of violence. I saw it first from the window of a downtown high-rise building where I had gone to be interviewed for a radio program. Fires seemed to erupt simultaneously in dozens of different locations. Everyone was taken by surprise. Observing the disaster, I thought of the burning of Atlanta in the film *Gone With the Wind*.

A short while later I was inside my home in the Silver Lake residential area not far from downtown L.A., watching the riots on TV. When I walked outside my door, I felt cinders falling on my face and hands. Helicopters began to fly over my house, making a deafening noise that further demonized the situation.

Then I moved inside again to watch what was happening on television. The situation was surreal. What sense could I make of this? Destruction and death on a vast social scale made me feel numb, helpless, and disoriented.

In my previous experience, death had been a singularly individual matter. My father's death stood out prominently.

My dad was someone who had struggled through a hard life. Finally, it seemed, he had learned to give up control before his death. An alcoholic with a legacy of two broken families and several failed work enterprises, he had quit drinking and become an amiable, wise, outgoing man who also had a wonderfully caring new wife. At this time, I had an opportunity to get to know my dad for the first time. When he died, he was no longer a stranger to me.

Observing my dad for the last time stretched out in a casket, I scarcely recognized him. His face was puffy and rouged. He was without the gigantic spark of life that had animated him in such a special way. Always I had found his humor a delight, his charm a balm.

A young priest, I read the burial office for him, standing above the casket at the foot of the chancel in a chapel. Later, at the cemetery, I committed his body ashes to ashes, dust to dust. My father's body was placed beside that of his father.

In the ensuing years I remembered his face in the casket. It was a mask. My father had already departed, that was clear. I knew there would be no point in kissing his cheek or touching his body in order to communicate. I was proud of him for finally making sense of his life, fighting a good fight, and getting himself ready for a valiant departure into the unknown.

I was a boy when I had my first encounter with death. It meant separation and loneliness for me, and seemed intolerably unfair. Laddie, my collie, was just about the best pal a kid in junior high ever had. Laddie went for a run one morning. He didn't come back home. I cried my eyes out. I looked virtually everywhere for him. Then somebody found his body on a street. He had been hit by a car. Damn it, I wondered, why did death have to take him? I hated death. Death hurt me a lot and seemed an insolent stranger.

Growing older, I thought about death from time to time. One was when I was seated in a doctor's office, waiting for my annual checkup. How lucky would I be this time? Magazines stacked on a table appeared dull, worn, and uninviting. I knew the doctor would want a urine specimen and a nurse would stick a needle in my arm to draw blood. Would they find something wrong? Would I have to go to a hospital? Would I have much time left?

Something like this has got to be a near universal experience. In his novel *A Single Man,* Christopher Isherwood showed how two men in a relationship dealt with the subject of death in a conversational, informal, funny, and serious way: "They talked about everything that came into their heads—including death, of course, and is there survival, and, if so, what exactly is it that survives. They even discussed the relative advantages and disadvantages of getting killed instantly and of knowing you're about to die."

I ran across death on television and in newspapers. I tended to find it morose, a bit heavy going and on the dark side, self-indulgent, set in its ways, and with an ego to burn. I felt that once it had made up its mind, it wouldn't be easy to change it. It was evident death could be cruel, demanding, unforgiving, obdurate, and imperious.

It occurred to me that I had worked hard all my life for security, sharpened my skills, developed a fine resume. From what I could discern, all these things would become meaningless.

What would happen to my body after I died? I wished my sense of humor could stay with me. I realized I had better start to detach myself from a total preoccupation with my body now, in order to get used to my future. Quit making a big deal of aches and pains, and sometimes making my own body the center of the universe. Was there a deeper lesson here? Could I live more easily on Earth, easing into a deeper relationship with my soul?

The afterlife sometimes seemed a bit like walking on the moon or reaching a distant planet. Would we be consciously reunited with others who had departed before us? Could we take a fast look back at earth and quickly size up everything? Yet we probably would be preoccupied with an entirely new and different focus and agenda.

As I grew older, sometimes when I listened to a favorite piece of music, it occurred to me it might be the last time I would hear it in a symphony hall or an opera house. Might this be my last visit to a foreign country or a city? If I were looking at something for the final time, could I invest a passionate intensity in the act? It seemed to me I wanted memory to burn forever in my consciousness, linger like a whispered word, continue to arouse longing and feeling in me.

But clearly, death represented ultimate and complete change. Was I afraid of change? I saw that it was present in the change from birth to maturity, in the seasons, in people, in history, in growing old. Could I try to stay open to new ideas? Cultivate curiosity? Reach a point where I desired to be a genuine part of change? If I did this, I might no longer have to be afraid of death.

Through the years of my life I had encounters with death in the deaths of friends. Jenny was adventurous, artistic, and fun-loving. I was surprised to discern beneath her gaiety how deeply prepared she was to depart this life. She had no fear. Jenny did not hold back from death. She greeted it with the same bravado and energy with which she had always welcomed life.

I saw Gary for the final time in the AIDS ward of the county hospital. He had developed retinitis and had started to see black spots before his eyes. Pulling up his bedshirt, he showed me the catheter that had been placed in his chest for medication. Gary was thirty-five when he died. While he had a passion for life, Gary welcomed death as a release from suffering.

Gary had been a landscape architect who was in the habit of calling the wildflower hotline to find out what areas of the county were in bloom. When he found spectacular views of hills full of wildflowers, he would stop his truck and explore their patches of color. I wondered if he might find the equivalent of gardens and wildflowers, in eternity.

Any former battles about being Number One and refusing to give up control were not in evidence in these friends whom I saw as they prepared to meet death. Sarah lay on her bed in a retirement home. Eighty-nine years old, she greeted me with a warm smile. On her nightstand I saw photographs of her late husband, her children and grandchildren. As always, she wore a colored ribbon in her hair. She talked animatedly, her mind straying to old memories. I sensed that Sarah was somehow aware this was to be our final visit together. Afterward, I recalled with affection that she talked about dying as a blessing and a doorway opening.

Virginia was a friend whom I had known since I was a boy. She was ten years older than I. Luck had deserted her, she was broke, and lived in a rambling, scarred old apartment. I had no idea my visit would be my goodbye to her.

She was as regal and indomitable as ever. This, despite the fact she had had a stroke, walked with a cane, and was ill. Virginia invited me to dinner at a McDonald's near her home. When we walked inside, it instantly became Buckingham Palace. She ordered a cheeseburger for me as if it were chateaubriand. Everybody treated her as if she were Queen Elizabeth II. I drank a coke, but it seemed to be cabernet sauvignon.

Virginia at sixty-five was a strikingly handsome woman. She carried on a conversation with me as if we were seated in the state dining room. Her long earrings reflected the light from a neon sign. Dessert? We would have a slice of pie with ice cream. I can still hear her sophisticated voice as she told wonderful stories, see her laughing eyes.

Our goodbye was a lovely one. A few weeks later I received a letter notifying me she had died. I felt sure Virginia had greeted death with confidence, laughter, and assurance. These seemed good qualities to take into eternity.

As I saw my friends face death, I increasingly wondered how I would do it. I realized the depth of sacrifice and surrender that would be required of me to enter into eternity. I had not yet learned sufficiently how to let go. In so many areas of life I found myself still struggling to hold onto control. I still cared too much about what other people thought, worldly trophies, and the illusion of security. Would I be prepared to give up all these things and step unencumbered and free into the promise of a completely new life of the soul?

Meanwhile, I caught sight of my own possible death, my own mortality, from time to time. One night when I was on an airplane in a blizzard, it seemed to come close. One thing was indisputably clear: The matter was completely beyond my control. The plane circled an intended landing site, an airport far below. Out of my window I could see nothing but swirling snow. A half-hour became an hour. An hour became an hour and a half. Every so often the pilot announced in an impersonal voice that there was nothing to report. I felt as if I were afloat on a tiny raft upon an angry sea with mountainous waves and a school of sharks.

A feeling of repressed hysteria grew in the cabin. I devoured the pages of a paperback, alternating this with prayer and meditation, as the plane engaged in sweeping turns, over and over again. Never had I felt closer to death's actual presence. It was uncomfortable, scary, and a bit exhilarating. It made me realize how unready for death I was; I needed to grow far closer to it, get more intimately acquainted, do better homework, make a friend of death. That night I didn't think it was fair of death to take advantage of our weak position. To death's merit, it didn't.

Then, I found myself even closer to death one morning when I was driving my car on a highway. Suddenly, blinded by snow swirling in front of my eyes, I saw another car. It was right in front of me. The cars crashed. My car was hurled along the icy road, out of control; then it landed in a ditch, overturned and spun.

I was thinking: *I'm going to die, I don't want to die, but I can't help dying now; it's out of my hands. What a dirty trick to die now. I hope it will be quick.* After that, there was total silence, and I struggled, groping for my leg, and my face: *Am I alive, am I here, am I whole?*

I was amazed and happy to find that I was. Now, after many, many years, numerous brushes with death, and a journey that has seemed as long and fraught with danger as that of Ulysses, it occurs to me that we can make our peace with death if we make our peace with life.

Since death is a part of life, why demonize it? If we learn to live honestly, openly, creatively, and hopefully, there is no reason we cannot die the same way.

CHAPTER 8

Make Our Peace

When an acquaintance died recently, I was told he died a disappointed and very angry man, unsatisfied, unforgiving, his soul gnarled in unresolved frustrations and rage. This saddened me. I thought: What a horrible way to die.

But of course, that is also the way he *lived*.

I remember when I lived that way too. I thought I saw a potential murderer, ready to stab me, behind every shadow. I trusted no one; after all, who knew what evil lurked in any supposedly human heart? In my frantic race to be Number One, I could not let down my guard for a single moment. I recall this existence as an extension of hell.

It is also a denial of life. Life remains the best show in town. It is wonderful—filled with mystery, tears, laughter, failure, success, hate, love, and redemption.

Each one of us has noble characteristics, dignity, and spiritual depth. We are also earthy creatures with human appetites, vanities, egos and, from time to time, wonderful humor. In given circumstances, we're a scream. Ego can produce belly laughs; so can sex, money, and politics. The emperor is funny (especially without clothes), and so are the peasants.

Although Hitler couldn't laugh at himself, Charlie Chaplin could laugh at him in *The Great Dictator.* And then, so could we. Erich Fromm pointed out that an element of humor was essential for survival in the deadening experience of the concentration camp, affirming the resiliency of the human spirit.

We can laugh at life. We can also laugh at death, at the stereotype of the "Grim Reaper," conjuring up Halloween-like images of scary masks, paper-maché skeletons, and shrouded creatures. Always I have found religion (and matters related to religion) funny as well as serious. I never doubted the relationship of the human comedy to the divine comedy. Author Thomas Moore, in *Care of the Soul,* argues for a broad vision of life: "It takes a broad vision to know that a piece of the sky and a chunk of the earth lie lodged in the heart of every human being, and that if we are going to care for that heart we will have to know the sky and the earth as well as human behavior." It seems to me we have to look at the human experience in widely varied ways, always cherishing a sense of humor on a par with faith itself.

As a kid and later a teenager, I hung around the church a lot. I was there Sunday mornings, sang in the choir when I was a boy, served as an acolyte later, and then came back Sunday nights for church suppers and meetings. I was very religious, but unfailingly saw church life in a context of opposites: ceremonial pomp vs. spiritual simplicity; clergy egos and careerism vs. the example of Jesus' humility and sacrifice; big church endowments vs. poverty on the streets; elaborate church buildings vs. Jesus' birth in a manger; spiritual hypocrisy vs. God's absolute truth; racism, sexism and homophobia in high places vs. God's inclusiveness and unconditional love; and churchianity vs. Christianity.

So, as a youth, I was both a loyal follower and a critic. The combination seemed natural, honest, and necessary. The wild, rich humor of the church came home to me on an evening in 1938 when Orson Welles produced his fateful *War of the Worlds* broadcast about an imaginary Martian invasion of Earth. By a sinister coincidence, that night two high school friends and I attended a supper at a midwestern cathedral, and we hatched a plot.

Bored and seeking excitement, we gave our testosterone free rein after we concocted a plan to climb up into the bell tower after everybody else had departed. We would ring the cathedral bells! It seemed an innocent lark that couldn't hurt anybody. We hid in the sanctuary until the cathedral's doors were bolted, lights were turned off, and voices drifted away into the night.

What we didn't know was that Welles had begun the broadcast of his classic program that would shortly result in mass terror. As the three of us moved swiftly through the cathedral's dark interior, we found the door leading to the bell tower. The stairs were narrow and winding. Unknown to us, the city was locked in deadly fear. To all intents and purposes, Martians had landed. Police stations were swamped with desperate calls. Many people were in the streets.

This was the moment we rang the bells. Those people who had held back, clinging to rational behavior, now leapt headlong into a crisis mode. The three of us, breathless with excitement and self-congratulation, were making our way hilariously down the winding stairs when we heard the sound of police sirens. They seemed to be drawing closer. We ran into the cathedral sanctuary mere footsteps ahead of a small army of police. As we crouched behind the bishop's throne in dark shadows, it seemed to us that the separation of church and state was in jeopardy at that moment. As the police raced up the stairway to the bell tower, we fled through the cathedral's herb garden to the safety of our homes.

After that, I could never regard religion without a sense of humor. The sheer drama of the church's life was compelling, especially its behind-the-scenes soap operas. *The War of the Roses* was a minor skirmish, I later learned, in comparison with a battle to elect a bishop.

In college I went wild, rebelled against the church, and assumed I had become an atheist. Outrageous things seemed to happen to me when (like a moth attracted to a flame) I visited a church. One Christmas Eve I went to a midnight eucharist where an elderly priest was the celebrant. He intoned parts of the service. Apparently he was rather deaf and unable to hear the harrowing sounds emanating from outside the church, where a stray dog began to howl in response to him. I started to shake uncontrollably, sobbing with laughter, but I was trapped in the middle of a crowded pew and could not get out.

Before ten years had passed, I had made a decision to enter the Episcopal priesthood. It wasn't long before I intoned parts of the eucharist myself. I wondered: Did a young man or woman, rebelling against the church and seated in a pew, find my performance amusing? Did a musical dog stand waiting outside an open church window, prepared to howl?

A sense of humor about spiritual matters still assists me as I contemplate my own perceptions of life and death. This has led me to be absolutely clear about the ritual surrounding my own rendezvous with death. I emphatically refuse a dour funeral devoid of gaiety, with tear-jerker hymns and sad people costumed for a solemn or funeral rite. No. This is the stuff of Greek tragedy. I want my ritual to be warm, touching, laced with moments of genuine passion, and executed with taste and beauty.

People whom I love, and who love me, need to be involved in its preparation. To get up and say what they feel about my life, our community, where we've been together, and how to discern meaning out of everything we've shared. A tape of a Billie Holiday song might be good. And great organ music to stir and startle people, carrying them deep into themselves, and releasing them into a vision of hope and transcendence. Then afterwards, hot food, cold drink, and heartfelt reminiscence.

The message of it all? Moving on with joy, in hope, surrounded by love. I find Sogyal Rinpoche's *The Tibetan Book of Living and Dying* immensely helpful in this regard. He points out that most people, lacking faith in an afterlife, experience life deprived of ultimate meaning. Such a short-term vision results in a brutal world, lacking compassion. He says that at the moment of death "the ordinary mind and its delusions die, and in that gap the boundless sky-like nature of our mind is uncovered." So, in his view, "it is vital for us all to familiarize ourselves with the nature of mind while we are still alive."

I believe there are certain definite steps we can take now in order to live more fully in the present moment, and also prepare for the moment of our departure into the next phase of our destiny with God.

If there is a key to our personal mystery, we should allow people to have it, so they can understand us better.

Learn to laugh at our own complexity, even share and analyze it with others. Learn to communicate in nonverbal ways. When we use words, have them say what we mean.

An awful example of just the opposite occurred one summer when I was a boy, with my parents at a gilt-edged hotel in the Adirondacks. Everything was very proper. The night we were invited to dine at the table of the hotel manager (the equivalent of the captain's table at sea), he began to regale us with stories of guests who stole items from their rooms, including towels and a spoon or knife from room service. When he became quite irate about this, it seemed to make me thoughtlessly proud of my cleverness. "All our towels at home are hotel towels," I announced solemnly. The manager's face froze. Conversation ceased. I realized I was at the center of attention. How glorious. "*And,*" I added, "all our spoons are hotel spoons." The evening was in shambles. My parents were socially embarrassed because, as everyone knows, children speak only the truth. Upon our return home several days later, I was shown our sole hotel spoon, boxed and ready to be returned by mail. Alongside it was our single hotel towel, torn and faded. I had done something seriously wrong. I had used communication to hurt people, and lied.

Another definite step we can take now is to act in freeing ways. Avoid rigidity. Speak to someone who appears forbidding. Tell the truth. Make a telephone call we have been afraid to make. Break a heavy silence. Place on paper a letter that has long been written in our mind. Ask the hard question. Even try to do what is clearly impossible for us.

In 1969, the war in Vietnam stretched on. Bombing continued unabated in its fury. Forty men and women, members of a peace fellowship, decided to conduct a Peace Mass in a crowded corridor of the Pentagon in Washington, D.C., as an act of protest and a prayer for peace. I was designated as the preacher and, as I said the words "The salt has lost its flavor," a police officer's voice rang out antiphonally, "You are under arrest." We boarded a bus to jail. We had done what we believed was necessary. It seemed nearly impossible—but not quite. I was glad we had acted in a freeing way.

In order to live more fully, we can take significant risks. Even, at certain moments, risk everything. What is there to save? Will we take it into the grave? Trappings of success have a way of deceptively masking unhappiness and the absence of fulfillment. What appears to be a failure often is the best teacher we'll have. In this world of present shock and rapid change, material security is the most ironic illusion. So why sell our soul for it?

Security, or a symbol of it, loomed large in my consciousness one day in 1996 as I confronted the awesome task of moving out of my office. After fifteen years there. But before moving, I had to empty it. There were pictures. File cabinets filled with papers. Books. Every kind of personal remembrance. I felt a bit like a bear that had long occupied a beloved cave, comfortable and safe. I found myself momentarily paralyzed. I just sat there, incapable psychologically and physically of cleaning out the office. Stripping it of every vestige of my presence. Saying goodbye, walking out, and closing the door behind me. When a friend said, "You've *got* to do it, and *now*," my focus shifted abruptly. I got the message, shaped up, did the job, and that was that. However, I fiercely resisted this small death. It seemed so hard to change. It required all my courage, resourcefulness, and energy.

In order to live more fully in the present, and prepare for our ultimate departure, we can strive to be more open and vulnerable. We needn't worry about what other people think. (Most of them are thinking about themselves.) We should laugh uproariously if we feel like it. Go to a park and ride a swing, whether we are ten or seventy. Cry if we are moved and wish to. Respond with the fullness of our being to a poem, the sound of the wind, or the beauty of a cello.

In love, we must hold nothing back. Give ourselves completely. Accept the other without reservation. Nurture love with kindness, *spices,* and gratitude. We shouldn't limit love. Some see it only in an erotic framework, others under a label of familial responsibility. We must be sure to include friendship, and cultivate it. When we stretch outward from a one-on-one relationship to make a network of connections with people, our sense of the universe becomes broader and, at the same time, more inclusive. When life is more fully shared, this moves us from selfish, passive withdrawal to being activated and involved with one another.

I absorbed a broader sense of the universe because of my Jewish grandfather. Since he had died before I was born, I never had the opportunity to know him. Yet I knew he was a part of my life. His heritage somehow summoned me, nurtured me, and affected me deeply. One day, in my fifties, I stood before the Western Wall in Jerusalem, my forehead pressed against an ancient stone; I believed that, by some strange twist of destiny, I also stood there for him. During my visit to Jerusalem I was received by an elderly, distinguished Jewish theologian. He knew that he was meeting an Episcopal priest from the United States who had written a book entitled *Are You Running with Me, Jesus?* I wondered what sense he made of that. Our meeting was friendly but formal. Suddenly, I glanced at my watch and realized I was running late for another appointment. "I've got to run," I exclaimed. The theologian didn't miss a beat when he responded, laughing, "God has placed a curse on you for writing that book. You will have to run forever." I fondly remember our meeting, especially when I am harassed, stressed, and running.

Since no one is an island, we need to quit acting like one. We must reach out for help, ask for it humbly, and admit our need. When help is given, we should accept it tenderly. When we perceive need in someone else, we must offer help immediately, simply, fully, and without feeling superior. Interact with the stranger who enters the orbit of our lives. All of us are affected by the common good, the common ill. Survival means banding together; justice requires it.

I remember the summer of 1964 when I worked as a civil rights volunteer on voter registration in rural Mississippi. One evening I sat in a country shack that was the home of an elderly African American man. He and his family had long been victims of a repressive society that not only denied them basic human rights, but seemed determined to call into question their very God-given humanity. This man had struggled for freedom all his life, yet had seen few evidences of it. He told me: "You see this watch? They can destroy it and the watch factory too, but they can't destroy time. They can kill me and wipe out my family, but they can't stop the freedom movement."

You *can't* kill the dream. It has an organic resistance to all the devised methods of killing. Attempts to murder a dream, in fact, vastly prolong its life. When a number of dreamers share their hopes and visions, forming a community of hope and commitment, the result is known as *the dream*. We are grateful to dreamers who went before us and shared *the dream* of love, peace, and freedom.

It is important for us to recognize that personal and social spheres of life have been thrust together, literally forcing a new kind of wholeness upon us. We have the opportunity to make our lives, our common life, the best anyone ever knew; even to become what humankind always wished and strove for through its ages of darkness and epiphanies of light. In a distant moment, a future earthling or a visitor from outer space may observe remnants of our life, and exclaim: "They were truly our sisters and brothers. We wish we could have known them."

Our challenge is to honor the present. While we are here, our lives can either be unhappy, self-destructive, unproductive, and lacking fire, *or* celebratory, loving, creative, and filled with spiritual energy.

Choose.

CHAPTER 9

Letters to Death

I wish that people did not feel the need to equate death with gloom, even despair. I find that I'm increasingly aware of a sense of excitement and anticipation about moving forward. Taking a further step of the spirit. Progressing into eternity. It seems the best way to prepare is to be fully alive, welcome joy and laughter, enjoy play and ecstasy in the divine comedy, and cultivate a passion for life.

We are dying as well as living all the time. On the basis of this, I can identify with Carlos Castaneda's Don Juan, who recognized death as "eternal companion." I yearn for a strong spiritual motivation to move me, scare the hell out of me when necessary, kick me lovingly in the butt, grant me great visions, and keep me from letting my life die before I do.

I hope I'll have few regrets when death comes. I would like to walk away hand in hand with death, feeling that I have struggled faithfully with the key issues that presented themselves to me. I hope that I will not cry or whine for more time. If I have used my time for love, and am eager to find what lies ahead, I won't have to.

Over the past ten years, it has helped me a great deal—as I tried to sort out my feelings and beliefs about death, and reflect on them—to write in my journals a series of short letters to death. I have done this through varying moods and in the midst of changing experiences in my life. The letters range from whimsy to anger, serious reflection to irony. I have confronted my need to demythologize death as well as honor it, and experience mutuality with it while endeavoring to decrease some of the dreadful power of its overawing mystique.

Dear Death:

In a certain sense I find you exciting, glamorous, unpredictable, mercurial. You appear to have a wicked sense of humor, a side of irony, and a cultivated sophistication. Obviously, you've been everywhere, done everything, known everybody, that sort of thing. I can't imagine your being at a loss for words. I'm sure you could charm the royal jewels off the queen.

However, what about your dark side? You're uncompromising, unyielding, a projection of your own image over everything, and incapable (it seems) of intimacy. The small gesture might escape you. So might mercy, simple kindness, and tenderness when it is needed most. I wonder: Would you agree with me that you never learned to give more than you receive?

Dear Death:

I keep hearing about the idea of setting out upon a great adventure with you. But I wonder if you know how to camp out on a mountain or in a forest. Can you hike, or do you require a stretch limo?

Dear Death:

Do you feel I am being mean to you? Lacking in sensitivity and sympathy, even empathy? The truth is, you baffle me. Perhaps I am poking at your facade in order to get a reaction. What is it precisely that you desire from me?

Although I am boisterously here among the living, I've seen you cast a wistful glance toward me out of the corner of an eye. Aren't I better for you here than on the other side? For one thing, I play my role expertly. Frankly, I can't imagine being away from this world's stage that I know so well. Saying my lines, singing and dancing, performing in repertory. Reading tomorrow morning's newspaper, responding to a letter from a friend with a masterpiece in kind. Preparing the next memorable salad, seeing the new play or film that everybody's talking about, listening to opera broadcasts from the Met, watching the World Series or Wimbledon on TV. Setting a roaring fire in a grate on a rainy day.

Why do you want to separate me from these things? Can't you just leave me alone?

Dear Death:

I remember when you stole my joy, unforgivably, and I still can't forgive you now after all these years. You took away someone I loved. After your unannounced visit, reminders of our life together were everywhere. A coffee mug in the breakfast nook, a favorite cookbook, a wine glass, a stack of letters held together by a rubber band. A surprising glimpse of the morning sky through a window. An heirloom quilt on the bed, a recording, a book of poems, a plant. The city's bright lights in a nighttime urban scene.

I did not want to see people, I cried without warning, craved aloneness, and felt I could never be happy again. I had possessed such a small space of joy in the vast world. I felt it would take forever to pick up the fragments of my life.

You bastard. You broke my heart.

Dear Death:

Dying, you know, is much more threatening to me than you are.

What will my own demise be like? A peaceful last scene surrounded by friends? A violent accident? If I commit a murder, an electric chair? Suffering a heart attack all alone? Disappearing beneath a mighty ocean wave?

I realize I have little or no control over the circumstances. Control. This seems to be the key word here. The absence of control over one of the most significant moments in my entire life.

However, I can shape my attitude about it. I can prepare mentally, emotionally, and spiritually. I can be ready.

Dear Death:

You must be aware there's a good deal of erotic imagery in your persona. You're seen wearing so much black. Never mauve or turquoise or gold. Are you setting up an image of yourself in leather?

Judging by all reports, you have a voracious appetite for life. You've been likened to an orgasm. I guess you enjoy a sensuous nature, revel in exotic tastes, have more than a surface interest in "S and M," and bring a touch of extended foreplay to numerous encounters.

But it seems to me you're too driven. I think you may need to slow down and lighten up. Relax. Be more laid back. You may be fine at sex, but do you know anything about love?

Dear Death:

If (as it appears) we're going to become acquainted sooner or later, let me tell you some things about myself.

I like to eat cold cereal for breakfast. (Eggs only one morning each week.)

I read a good newspaper first thing in the morning with my coffee.

I shun daytime TV.

I opt for cremation, with my ashes scattered.

I need someone to water the plants after I'm gone.

For lunch, half a sandwich (tuna?) is fine with me.

No more coffee during the day. (I'm cutting down on caffeine).

I care that my friends get a neat, unscary, maybe slightly endearing announcement of my demise. (First class mail will do.)

I hope that someone will remember to disconnect the phone, and cancel the *New Yorker,* the *Nation,* and *Opera News.*

I like a cup of tea in the afternoon. No sweets.

A glass of Merlot with dinner.

Remember my habits: I'm rather shy, not terribly

gregarious, don't enjoy crowds, and prefer people one-on-one.

For C.D.s, I want one more Erroll Garner, one less Vivaldi.

I prefer to sleep at nights with a window cracked open.

Dear Death:

What an irony it is. I've listened seemingly forever to endless fearsome stories about your importance, dread, and the major role you play in human affairs. But what if you're not needed at all? This fact would plummet your carefully constructed myth of self-promotion into the most outrageous expose of fabrication, wouldn't it? You'd be revealed as a braggart, even a phony, and I would be liberated instantly from your mystique.

Instead of your feeling so important, perhaps you should feel impotent. You're only an instrument. You serve a needed purpose. You're like a dentist, a sanitation worker, a flight attendant, a newspaper vendor, a lawyer, or an usher. You're a messenger. You're not the message.

Dear Death:

This is going to happen to *me*!

I'm going to die. All the experiences and meanings of my entire life will be summed up in this singular act, and outrageously abbreviated in a well-meaning but flawed obituary.

I can't believe it.

Yet at last I face the implications of a question I've asked forever: Can I find fulfillment and peace in the present moment? Is it possible for me to leave behind the past, cut off anticipation of a future I try to define, and stay completely in the now?

If not, my dying would seem to make little sense. It would seem redundant and flat.

In the moment of dying I hope to be fully centered in God, suffused by love, and to feel a trust in Jesus Christ so intense that it transcends past and future alike.

Dear Death:

Hope and faith have at long last broken through my defense system. At last, I feel no need to justify myself, be understood, or try to explain anything.

Regrets are smoothed out like old wrinkles. I feel mellow about old enemies.

I am simply who I am. Yes, I accept my sins and failures that have bruised and hurt other people as well as myself. I also accept forgiveness for them, and do this most gratefully. I stand in wonderment.

Now I am ready to let go.

I embrace love and open my heart to the holy.

I am enveloped in joy.